JESUS

Jesus: A 30 Day Devotional

ISBN 10: 1-931899-46-8

ISBN 13: 978-1-931899-46-8

Copyright © Basic Gospel 2020

Published by Basic Gospel, Inc.

Introduction

Jesus Christ is Christianity. He is the foundation, the chief cornerstone.

His story is the story of the Bible. From Genesis to Revelation, God gives to us His testimony concerning His Son.

Many people miss this truth. They miss Jesus. The Apostle Paul was like that. He read and studied the Bible diligently with the hope that in its pages he would find eternal life. He missed the central truth that life is in the Son.

Instead of receiving Jesus as the Messiah, Paul blasphemed his name and sought to destroy the church. All that changed in an instance. He met the real Jesus. From that day forward, *"that I may know Him"* was his singular ambition. In light of the surpassing greatness of knowing Christ, everything else paled in comparison.

In his high priestly prayer, Jesus defined eternal life. It is this: *"that they may know You, the only true God, and Jesus Christ whom You have sent"* (John 17:3). Eternal life is knowing Jesus Christ, the Great I AM.

We pray this devotional will inspire you to "know Him." And that in knowing him, you will discover that he is enough…in fact, that *he is everything*.

Jesus Christ

is

Christianity.

He is the

foundation,

the chief

cornerstone.

Day 1 – In the Beginning: The Word

 ## Hear it

In the beginning was the Word, and the Word was with God, and the Word was God…And the Word became flesh and dwelt among us, and we have seen his glory, glory as of the only Son from the Father, full of grace and truth (John 1:1, 14 ESV).

 ## Believe It

Who is Jesus?

John makes it clear in his opening line in his gospel account.

Jesus is God.

He was in the beginning as the Word. He was with God. He was God.

Everything came to be through him. He is the creator, the one who in the beginning spoke the world into existence.

In him was life, the life that was the light of men.

This is Jesus.

Some would have you believe that he is merely a prophet, or a good moral teacher, or an example to follow. But they are not talking about the real Jesus.

The Jesus the Bible speaks of is God of the universe, the all powerful, all knowing, almighty one.

At a point in time, he became flesh and blood and dwelt among us as the one full of grace of truth.

Almighty God became one of us in the person of Jesus Christ.

He showed up to give us grace, truth and life. None of which a prophet, or a moral teacher, or a good example could give us.

Only God can save us.

He has a name. Jesus!

 ## Live It

Jesus Christ is God. The world may not know him as God. But you know the truth. And you have come to know Him as the God of grace, the one who gave you eternal life.

Day 2 – The Image of the Invisible God

 Hear it

He is the image of the invisible God, the firstborn of all creation. For by him all things were created, in heaven and on earth, visible and invisible, whether thrones or dominions or rulers or authorities–all things were created through him and for him. And he is before all things, and in him all things hold together. And he is the head of the body, the church. He is the beginning, the firstborn from the dead, that in everything he might be preeminent (Colossians 1:15-18 ESV).

 Believe It

Every January millions of people resolve to lose weight. Exercise and healthy eating for the new year. For many on this path, healthy eating includes a daily smoothie.

To make a smoothie, you take the healthiest items from various food groups and blend them together in a blender. The key word is blend. This works well for smoothies. It doesn't work well when it comes to religion and philosophy.

Colosse was a perfect example. They took all they deemed good and beneficial from various religions and philosophies and mixed them together.

They chased after empty and deceptive philosophies. They doubled down on the rules, the regulations and the religious rituals. They even fell prey to worshiping angels. To them, this seemed wise. But it proved to be a disaster.

That was Paul's point in his letter to the Colossians. You can't mix the things of this world with Jesus. You can't improve on who Jesus is or what he has done.

He wants you to know and believe this as well. He penned the clearest and most concise description of Jesus that you can find in the Word of God. Jesus is…

- the image of the invisible God

- the firstborn, which means the supreme being, over all creation

- the creator of all things in heaven and earth

- before all things, which means he has always been

- the one who holds all things together

- the head of the body

- the beginning, the original cause

- first born from the dead.

It's no wonder that Paul said Jesus is preeminent in all things.

This is Jesus. He stands alone. There is no one like him.

He is complete and sufficient in all things. In him are all the treasures of wisdom and knowledge.

Once you receive him, there is nothing more that you need.

Live It

This crazy world throws all kinds of ideas and philosophies at us...ways to achieve success, find happiness and peace, or feel confident and bold. On the surface, they all seem to have a measure of wisdom, or a hint of truth... something that promises to make you a better version of yourself.

The temptation is to mix these worldly ideas in with Christianity, with Jesus. Jesus stands alone. As for eternal life, forgiveness of sins and unconditional love, it is Jesus plus nothing. Rest today in his love and grace knowing that he is the preeminent one in your life.

Day 3 – The Radiance

 Hear it

Long ago, at many times and in many ways, God spoke to our fathers by the prophets, but in these last days he has spoken to us by his Son, whom he appointed the heir of all things, through whom also he created the world. He is the radiance of the glory of God and the exact imprint of his nature, and he upholds the universe by the word of his power. After making purification for sins, he sat down at the right hand of the Majesty on high... (Hebrews 1:1-3 ESV).

 Believe It

In the Old Testament, God delivered his word to the people through the prophets, men like Jeremiah and Daniel and Isaiah.

Moses was counted in that number as well. Now all of these prophets knew that one day another person would come on the scene who would deliver the complete revelation of God.

Moses said as much near the end of his life. He delivered this prophecy to the people:"The Lord your God will raise up for you a prophet like me from among you, from your brothers–it is to him you shall listen– " (Deuteronomy 18:15).

Another prophet was coming...one that outranked Moses...one that would deliver God's words of eternal life.

The writer of Hebrews identifies Jesus as this prophet. God has spoken to us today through him, the Son. He has delivered to us God's grace and truth.

Jesus stands above all the prophets of old. They, as one commentary described them, were merely mouthpieces. When Jesus spoke, it was God himself speaking.

Look at how the writer of Hebrews describes Jesus. He was appointed by the Father as the heir of all things, and it was through him the world came to be.

When Jesus speaks, it is no ordinary man speaking. This is God in human flesh…the radiance of the glory of God and the exact imprint of his nature. Jesus is one in essence and character with the Father and is the one who upholds the universe by his power.

God has not only spoken through Jesus, he brought about purification of sins through him.

Jesus died to take away the sins of the world. When his work was finished he sat down at the right hand of God the Father, the majesty on high.

God has spoken through Jesus. And the word is good news for you.

 ## Live It

Jesus is superior to the prophets of old in every way. As the writer of Hebrews wrote, let's pay much closer attention to what we have heard through him and experience the full measure of this great salvation that he has delivered to us in grace and truth.

Day 4 – A Savior

 # Hear it

And the angel said to them, "Fear not, for behold, I bring you good news of great joy that will be for all the people. For unto you is born this day in the city of David a Savior, who is Christ the Lord (Luke 2:10, 11 ESV).

 # Believe It

Who is Jesus?

He is the Savior…your Savior.

He is good news of great joy.

The people of Israel lived in anticipation of his birth. They knew he was to come. All the prophets testified as such.

Micah even pinpointed the place of his arrival as Bethlehem. But none of the people expected him to enter this world in such a humble and obscure setting.

As the angel had announced to Mary, *"And behold, you will conceive in your womb and bear a son, and you shall call his name Jesus. He will be great and will be called the Son of the Most High. And the Lord God will give to him the throne of his father David, and he will reign over the house of Jacob forever, and of his kingdom there will be no end"* (Luke 1:31-33).

He deserved a more fitting welcome. Yet, when he was born, because there was no room in the inn, Mary had to wrap him in swaddling clothes and lay him in a manger.

You would think that God would make the birth of his Son known to the King of Israel and the chief priests. Instead, God sent his angel to lowly shepherds in the nearby fields.

In their humble state, they saw the glory of God. As Luke wrote, it shone around them, and they were afraid.

The angel said to them, *"Fear not, for behold, I bring you good news of great joy that will be for all the people. For unto you is born this day in the city of David a Savior, who is Christ the Lord" (Luke 2:10, 11).*

As Savior, Jesus humbled himself and became one of us to save us from our sins. When we humbly welcome him for who he is, our Savior, then we too can see and share in the glory of God.

 Live It

Who is Jesus? He is your Savior. This is good news.

This is cause for great joy. Rejoice that he loved you and humbled himself to die for your sins and give you eternal life.

Day 5 – God With Us

 # Hear it

Behold, the virgin shall conceive and bear a son, and they shall call his name Immanuel (which means, God with us) (Matthew 1:23 ESV).

 ## Believe It

What is in a name? When it comes to Jesus, everything.

Jesus means savior. This was the name he was called. This is the name we call him. As the angel told Joseph, "She will bear a son, and you shall call his name Jesus, for he will save his people from their sins" (Matthew 1:21).

Jesus saved you from your sins. That's what he came to do.

But that is not his only name. The angel told Joseph that they will call him Immanuel. This name tells us who he is.

It means God with us. Jesus is God with us.

For Joseph, knowing Jesus's identity was the truth that set him free from his fear to take Mary as his wife. God with you…it's the truth that will set you free from your fears as well

God with man. This has always been God's desire. This is the way it was in the beginning. This is the way it is now in Christ.

He became flesh and blood and dwelt among us.

After his resurrection and ascension, he sent the Spirit to dwell in us. As Paul wrote in his letter to the Colossians, *"Christ in you, the hope of glory"* (Colossians 1:27).

Jesus saved you from your sins and he is now with you through the Holy Spirit.

It's a truth that proclaims to you everyday, "fear not."

Here is your confidence for daily living. Whatever life throws at you, God is with you. And his name is Jesus Christ.

 Live It

This world is a frightening place. But you know Jesus. His name matters. He saved you and now lives in you. And he promised he will never leave you.

Let this truth be your confidence to live boldly as a child of God resting fully in his presence.

Day 6 – A Son is Given

 # Hear it

For to us a child is born, to us a son is given; and the government shall be upon his shoulder, and his name shall be called Wonderful Counselor, Mighty God, Everlasting Father, Prince of Peace (Isaiah 9:6 ESV).

 # Believe It

God's word is the story of Jesus from beginning to end. It is God's testimony concerning his Son.

Jesus said as much in one of his conversations with the religious leaders. *"It is these [the Scriptures] that testify about me"* (John 5:39).

After his resurrection Jesus approached two of his disciples as they were walking on the road to Emmaus. Jesus, beginning with Moses and with all the prophets, "explained to them the things concerning himself in all the Scriptures" (Luke 24:27).

Wherever you turn in the Bible, both the Old and the New, you will read God's testimony about Jesus. You will discover who he is.

Isaiah gave a powerful description in his prophecy.

He is the child that was born, the Son that was given.

God said his name shall be called…

Wonderful Counselor.

Mighty God.

Everlasting Father.

Prince of Peace.

This is God's testimony concerning his Son.

He is your Wonderful Counselor.

He is your Mighty God.

He is your Everlasting Father.

He is your Prince of Peace.

This is Jesus, the one who rules and reigns in your life.

 ## Live It

God so loved you that he sent his Son into the world. You first met him as your Savior. He died for your sins and gave you life. Now he comforts you with his presence. He is your victory. He loves you with an everlasting love. He is your peace.

Next time you open the Bible, God will tell you more about his Son.

Day 7 – Make Him Known

 ## Hear it

No one has ever seen God; the only God, who is at the Father's side, he has made him known (John 1:18 ESV).

 ## Believe It

Why did Jesus come into the world? The Bible gives many answers. I like the one John gives in his gospel account. Jesus came into the world to make the Father known…to you.

Throughout human history, misinformation has spread far and wide about God. He is an angry God, a judgmental God, a vengeful God, a mean God, a violent God, a distant God, a "no matter what you do you will never please me" God. The list goes on and on.

None of these descriptions are true. Far from it. But they are held in the minds of people…minds that have never seen the truth about God in Christ. It's no wonder. The bible says the mind of the flesh is hostile toward God. It also says that at one time *"we were alienated from God and enemies in our mind because of our evil behavior"* (Colossians 1:21).

Through this mindset we make God look like a Picasso painting. It's our fear of punishment that paints such a distorted view.

This is why Jesus came into the world…to change our view of God…to show us the truth. He underscored this point emphatically when he said to Philip, *"Whoever has seen me has seen the Father"* (John 14:9).

When you have seen Jesus you know that God is love. This is the truth. It is a radical departure from all the lies of the world concerning God. Now through Christ, the truth about God has been deposited in your heart and mind.

And it changes everything.

For the world, the true essence of God is a mystery. The philosophers in Athens understood this to be so. They inscribed these words on an altar: *"To an unknown God"* (Acts 17:23). He is not unknown to you. Jesus Christ fulfilled his purpose by making God the Father known to you.

Here is the good news. Jesus continues that work in your life to grow your knowledge of God the Father and God the Son.

 Live It

In his first letter, the Apostle John wrote this: *"Beloved, let us love one another, for love is from God, and whoever loves has been born of God and knows God"* (1 John 4:7). Your love for others flows from this truth…you have been born of God and you know God.

You have something the world needs…the truth about God. Let them know that he is love. Help them see the glory of God in the face of Jesus Christ.

Day 8 – I AM

Hear it

Jesus said to them, "Truly, truly, I say to you, before Abraham was, I am" (John 8:58 ESV).

Believe It

When God called out to Moses from the burning bush, he said to him, "I have surely seen the affliction of my people...I know their sufferings, and I have come to deliver them..." (Exodus 3:7, 8).

God chose Moses to lead his people out of Egypt. Moses wasn't sure how the people would react to his leadership. He asked God, "If I come to the people of Israel and say to them, 'the God of your fathers has sent me to you' and they ask me, 'What is his name?' What shall I say to them?"

God responded, "I am who I am. Say this to the people of Israel: 'I am has sent me to you.'"

I Am. This is God's name. It's Yahweh (YHWH) in Hebrew. To the people of Israel, this name is holy, sacred, unspoken.

This *tetragrammaton* is the proper biblical name of God. It declares his essence. It means God will never be anything other than who he is...never changing and ever constant. This is God.

Some fifteen hundred years later in a contentious conversation with the Pharisees who were questioning his authority and identity, Jesus claimed the name of God as his own. *"Before Abraham was, I am."*

The religious leaders judged this as blasphemy. They picked up stones to stone him in accordance with the law. This proves they heard him loud and clear. There was no mistake that Jesus was claiming to be the great *I Am*.

In Moses' day, *I Am* showed up to deliver his people out of bondage. That was a foreshadowing of his ultimate work in Christ. He knows your afflictions and sufferings. He has heard your cries. Jesus came to set you free from sin and death. *"And when the Son has set you free, you are free indeed."*

Only the great *I Am* could do such a thing. The one who was, who is and who will be…never changing and ever constant in his love for you.

 ## Live It

Jesus is I Am. This is his essence, his nature. He will never be anything other than who he is. Which means you can count on him to be everything he is for you.

Day 9 – Bread of Life

Hear it

Jesus said to them, "I am the bread of life; whoever comes to me shall not hunger, and whoever believes in me shall never thirst (John 6:35 ESV).

Believe It

Five barley loaves and two fish is all the food the disciples could find. In Jesus's hands this was more than enough to feed the crowd which numbered 5,000 men plus women and children. After everyone ate, there was plenty of food leftover.

The crowd, amazed by this miracle, said, *"This is truly the prophet who is to come into the world."* At that moment, this crowd had every intention of taking Jesus by force and making him their king.

Jesus had other plans, a truth to tell them that would satisfy their spiritual hunger forever. So Jesus withdrew to the mountain alone.

The next morning, the crowd returned to the place where Jesus had fed them. When they realized Jesus wasn't there, they got in boats and crossed the sea to Capernauem.

Jesus knew why they followed him. They wanted more food. Jesus said to them, "Do not work for the food that perishes, but for the food which endures to eternal life..."

Okay Jesus, what are we supposed to do *"to be doing the works of God?"*

It's a good question. Have you ever asked this of God?

Jesus responded, "This is the work of God, that you believe in him whom he has sent."

Why him? Why Jesus?

His answer is unlike any that has ever been offered. Jesus claimed to be the One whom God had sent. He proclaimed, *"I am the Bread of Life, whoever comes to me shall not hunger"* (John 6:35).

Again in verse 51 he boldly stated *"I am the living bread that came down from heaven. If anyone eats of this bread, he will live forever."*

For many of the people who followed him, this was a hard saying. Too much for them to grasp. John wrote that they *"turned back and no longer walked with him"* (John 6:66).

For Peter and the other eleven, Jesus's words were *"the words of eternal life"* (John 6:68).

Eternal life is in Christ. He is the bread of life. He alone satisfies our spiritual hunger.

What about you? Have you received the bread of life?

 Live It

"I am the bread of life." This is a radical claim and for many hard to take. But, it is true. Jesus Christ is the one whom God sent. Everyone who believes in him lives forever. Thank God today that your spiritual hunger has been satisfied through faith in Jesus.

Day 10 – The Light of the World

 Hear it

Again Jesus spoke to them, saying, "I am the light of the world. Whoever follows me will not walk in darkness, but will have the light of life" (John 8:12 ESV).

 Believe It

Have you ever been on a spelunking expedition? I did through Mammoth Cave in Kentucky. It was quite the experience.

Our guide led us through one passageway that was so narrow and shallow we had to crawl on our bellies to get through it.

At the other end was a huge cavern. The only light in that cavern was from the lights on our helmets.

On our guide's signal, we all turned our lights off. The darkness was overwhelming. I could not see my hand in front of my face. The darkness unsettled all of us. We were paralyzed in place, afraid to take a step in any direction.

That's the kind of darkness we lived in before knowing Christ…a darkness that paralyzed us and left us feeling unsettled and lost.

In that cavern, we were able to turn our lights on and regain our bearings. That's not the case when it comes to spiritual darkness. As Paul wrote, *"you were formerly darkness"* (Ephesians 5:8).

We are not without hope. Light has come into the world. Jesus is that light. He boldly proclaimed, *"I am the light of the world. Whoever follows me will not walk in darkness, but will have the light of life."*

Believe in him, and you will not stay in darkness. You will have the light of life. You can move forward confident and sure in the light of his love.

 ## Live It

Darkness is not the place to be. That's where you were... unsettled and lost. Then Jesus entered in and rescued you. He placed you into his wonderful light. Now you are light in the Lord. As Peter wrote, *"proclaim the excellencies of him who called you out of darkness into his marvelous light"* (1 Peter 2:9 ESV).

Day 11 – The Door

 Hear it

I am the door. If anyone enters by me, he will be saved and will go in and out and find pasture (John 10:9 ESV).

 Believe It

One of the popular game shows on TV is *Let's Make A Deal*. Make the right deal and you get a chance to win a big prize, which is behind either door number one, two, or three. It's a risk. Two of the doors are total busts. But guess right and the prize is yours.

That's the way many people think about happiness and contentment. Guess the right door the world offers, and these things are yours.

But that's not the case with abundant life. Jesus eliminated the guess work. He told you the door to pick. He said, *"I am the door. If anyone enters by me he will be saved and will go in and out and find pasture"* (John 10:9).

The world puts all kinds of doors in front of you. These doors entice with their offers…six steps to happiness or ten steps to successful living. You get the drift. But they are nothing but total busts.

The world offers, but it can't deliver.

But not Jesus. Anyone who enters by him is saved and finds pasture in him.

That's why he came into this world.

The thief comes to steal, kill and destroy. Jesus came that you might have life and have it to the full.

This life is for here and now…eternal life today. It's a quality of life the world knows nothing about.

If you've walked through the door, it's yours in abundance.

 ## Live It

Jesus Christ is the door that leads to life, true joy and happiness. He is the real deal. All that's in the world is imitation. All those worldly doors are impostors, nothing more than thieves and robbers.

You've entered eternal life through faith in Jesus Christ. You have the real thing. Now go out and enjoy His life to the full.

Day 12 – The Good Shepherd

 Hear It

I am the good shepherd. The good shepherd lays down his life for the sheep (John 10:11 ESV).

 Believe It

The 23rd Psalm is a wonderful passage filled with hope and comfort. It starts with these familiar words, *"The Lord is my shepherd. I shall not want."*

Jesus is that shepherd, the good shepherd.

He laid down his life for you. There is no greater love than this.

There are many impostors in the world who pretend to care about you. They are wolves in sheep's clothing. They don't care about you, only themselves.

They try to entice you to lead you astray. When trouble comes, they flee.

But not the good shepherd.

Jesus knows you and has committed himself to you. And you know him.

You heard his voice and you followed him. He gave you eternal life, and you will never perish. You are safe in his hand.

You can trust him in every situation knowing that he will never lead you astray.

Sheep need a shepherd.

Jesus Christ is your good shepherd, the shepherd and overseer of your soul.

 Live It

The world is not your friend. It does everything to lead you astray. When you were lost, you followed. But you heard another voice, the voice of Jesus. You recognized him as the one who genuinely loves and cares for you. You followed him and he gave you eternal life.

Keep listening. He will never lead you astray.

Day 13 – The Resurrection and the Life

 Hear It

Jesus said to her, "I am the resurrection and the life. Whoever believes in me, though he die, yet shall he live, and everyone who lives and believes in me shall never die. Do you believe this?" (John 11:25, 26 ESV).

 Believe It

Lazarus was ill. His sisters, Martha and Mary, sent word to Jesus to come quickly. They wanted Jesus to heal him like they had seen him do for so many others.

When Jesus got word, he said to his disciples, *"This illness does not lead to death. It is for the glory of God so that the son of God may be glorified through it."*

The people would soon find out what Jesus meant. They were going to see that Jesus has power over death. That's the good news, the heart and soul of Christianity.

When Jesus finally arrived, Lazarus had been dead for four days.

Martha went out to meet him and said to him, *"Lord if you had been here my brother would not have died."*

Martha had great hope that Jesus would heal Lazarus. But when he died her hope vanished. The same was true for Mary and the crowd that had gathered to grieve with them.

The idea that Jesus could raise him back to life never entered her mind.

Jesus said to her, *"Your brother will rise again."*

In the midst of that hopelessness, Jesus proclaimed, *"I am the resurrection and the life. Whoever believes in me though he die yet shall he live and everyone who lives and believes in me shall never die. Do you believe this?"*

Death is not a problem to God. Jesus was about to show this power.

Jesus, moved with compassion, said *"remove the stone."* Then he cried with a loud voice, *"Lazarus come forth."*

Lazarus walked out of his tomb, healed and fully alive. Jesus's glory, his power over death, had now been revealed for all to see.

This is the story of the gospel of Jesus Christ.

Jesus died, was buried, and was raised back to life. The same happened to you. You died in Christ, were buried with him through baptism, and then you were raised to walk in the newness of life.

You experienced that resurrection power the moment you believed.

 Live It

Christianity is not a self-improvement program. It's not a ten step program that helps you become a better version of yourself.

God takes people who are dead in sin and makes them alive together with Christ Jesus. This happens through the One who is the resurrection and the life.

Just as Jesus called Lazarus by name, He called you by name and raised you to walk in the newness of life. This is your story. This is what it means to participate in the good news of Jesus Christ.

Day 14 – The Way, the Truth, The Life

 ## Hear It

Jesus said to him, "I am the way, and the truth, and the life. No one comes to the Father except through me" (John 14:6 ESV).

 ## Believe It

Jesus Christ bridges the gap between life and death. We cross over through him. There is no other way.

Jesus said as much. *"I am the way, and the truth, and the life. No one comes to the Father except through me."*

Jesus Christ is not one of many ways to God. He is the way. It's that simple and that clear.

For many, this statement is offensive. Why? Its exclusive nature eliminates the possibility of another way to God.

The same applies to truth and life.

The way to God is through Jesus. The truth about God is bound up in Jesus. The life of God is found in Jesus.

Other philosophies and religions don't hold up. Any claim they make that there is more than one way to God misses the point. Our need is life. As Paul wrote in Ephesians 2:1, *"And you were dead in the trespasses and sins…"*

This is why Jesus came into the world, that you might have life. This life is in Jesus–nowhere else.

He is the way out of death into life–eternal life.

Live It

Jesus is God's plan A. There is no plan B. You either trust in him as the way, the truth and the life, or you remain dead in your trespasses and sins. Here is the good news. The day you trusted Jesus Christ, you crossed over from death to life through Him.

Day 15 – The Vine

 Hear It

I am the vine; you are the branches. Whoever abides in me and I in him, he it is that bears much fruit, for apart from me you can do nothing (John 15:5 ESV).

 Believe It

Every Christian wants a fruitful life. They want to be marked by love, joy, peace, patience, kindness, goodness, gentleness, faithfulness and self-control. But how? That's the question that mystifies so many believers.

The answer is found in Jesus's statement, *"I am the vine."*

He is the source of life. All the goodness of the Christian life flows from him to you.

Jesus is the creator. He created us in his image and likeness. Our life is derived from his. This makes sense.

Apart from him, life is a mess. Jesus said apart from him we can do nothing. Your life when you were lost and dead in sin confirms Jesus's statement. You were bearing fruit, just not the right kind. Back then you were abiding in the world, following its ways and living to gratify the desires of the flesh.

But now, you are in Christ. You are attached to the vine by grace through faith. You live in him. That's what it means to abide. You are connected to the source of life. Christ's life is flowing through you.

Our nature as humans is that of a branch. Branches don't produce fruit, they bear fruit. Now that you are attached to Christ, you will bear the fruit of his life.

Live It

Paul asked the believers in Galatia this question: *"After starting your Christian lives in the Spirit, why are you now trying to become perfect by your own human effort?* (Galatians 3:3 NLT). We can't bear fruit through human effort. That only frustrates and exasperates us.

We head down that wrong path because we have either forgotten that Jesus is the vine, or someone has taught us that human effort is the key to the Christian life.

If you feel frustrated with your Christian life, step back and ask yourself if you truly believe that Jesus is the vine. This will compel you to let go of human effort and re-shape your thinking to a simple life of trusting Jesus to produce the fruit of his life in you.

Day 16 – One

 Hear It

"I and the Father are one" (John 10:30 ESV).

 Believe It

Blasphemy under the law was a capital offense.

Leviticus 24:6 is clear on this point: *"Whoever blasphemes the name of the Lord shall surely be put to death. All the congregation shall stone him. The sojourner as well as the native, when he blasphemes the Name, shall be put to death."*

When Jesus made the statement, *"I and the Father are one,"* the Jews picked up stones to stone him. They were ready to carry out the law of Moses.

Jesus asked them to identify the good work he had done that justified their condemnation.

The Jews answered him, *"It is not for a good work that we are going to stone you but for blasphemy, because you, being a man, make yourself God"* (John 10:33).

They heard Jesus loud and clear. In his statement, Jesus claimed to be God, equal with the Father. This wasn't the first time they took offense at Jesus's claims about himself, and it wasn't the last.

Before Jesus was handed over to Pilate to be crucified, the High Priest asked, *"Are you the Christ, the Son of God?"* Jesus answered, *"I am"* (Mark 14:62). On hearing this answer, the high priest tore his clothes and said, *"You have heard his blasphemy."* The chief priests and council condemned him as deserving death.

Jesus's claims about himself would be blasphemous if they weren't true. But he is the Son of God. He and the Father are one. Which means you can believe what Jesus says.

Now that's important. Right before Jesus claimed to be one with the Father, he said: *"My sheep hear my voice, and I know them, and they follow me. I give them eternal life, and they will never perish, and no one will snatch them out of my hand. My Father, who has given them to me, is greater than all, and no one is able to snatch them out of the Father's hand"* (John 10:27, 28).

Jesus gave you eternal life. You will never perish. No one will snatch you out of his hands, or the Father's hand. You can believe this with utmost confidence because *"I and the Father are one."*

 Live It

Jesus and the Father are one. This is good news for you. Jesus's word is true and trustworthy. His word to you as a believer is that your salvation is secure. You are safe in his hands. As Charles Spurgeon said, "Believe it and be happy."

Day 17 – The Question

 Hear It

He said to them, "But who do you say that I am?" (Matthew 16:15 ESV).

 Believe It

Jesus was causing quite a stir. Great crowds were gathering everywhere he went. Some were there for his teaching. Others wanted a miracle. Regardless, they were curious about this man named Jesus. They began to talk about who he might be.

The disciples had their ears close to the talk. Jesus wanted to find out what they were hearing. He took the disciples to Caesarea Philippi, near the headwaters of the Jordan River, and he asked them, *"Who do people say that I am?"*

They told Jesus that some thought he was John the Baptist. Others said he was Elijah, or Jeremiah or one of the other prophets.

Then, in what was a pivotal moment for the disciples, Jesus turned the question on them. "What about you," he asked, *"Who do you say that I am?"* This is the most compelling and relevant question that has ever been asked.

Peter was the one who stood to answer. With confidence in his voice, he declared, *"You are the Christ, the Son of the living God."* This wasn't information Peter figured out on his own. God the Father revealed this truth to him.

And it wasn't just a fact that Peter learned. This revelation was the headwaters of something new and revolutionary. Jesus put it this way: *"On this rock, I will build my church."* The foundation of the church had its beginnings right here – the confession that Jesus Christ is the Son of the Living God.

Jesus is both Lord and God. Christianity begins and carries on eternally with him.

 ## Live It

The day you believed you made the confession that Jesus is the Son of God.

Not only is this the starting point of your faith in Christ, it is the truth that calms your heart and mind in life's most trying times. The Son of God lives in you. He is bigger than any trial that life brings your way. You don't have to bear these problems yourself. Release them to Jesus knowing that he is big enough to work the situation together for your good.

What about you? Who do you say that Jesus is?

Day 18 – The Invitation

 Hear It

Come to me, all who labor and are heavy laden, and I will give you rest. Take my yoke upon you, and learn from me, for I am gentle and lowly in heart, and you will find rest for your souls. For my yoke is easy, and my burden is light" (Matthew 11:28-30 ESV).

 Believe It

"Weary and burdened." This describes way too many Christians today.

They are trying as hard as they know how to live right and to do right. But it is all through human effort. It's an exhausting life.

Maybe you've felt that way or are feeling that way right now.

Here is the good news. Human effort is not a part of the Christian life. There is not a single verse in the Bible that tells you to try harder, or do more.

The message of the Bible is Jesus.

He extends the invitation to come unto him.

This is where Christianity differs from every other religion or worldly philosophy. Jesus offers rest for the soul.

He has done all the work necessary to make you right in God's sight. He finished the work. When he did, he sat down at the right hand of God the Father.

Jesus put it this way in his high priestly prayer: *"I have brought you glory on earth by finishing the work you gave me to do. And now, Father, glorify me in your presence with the glory I had with you before the world began"* (John 17:4, 5).

There is nothing more to do concerning your sins. Jesus did it all. This means you can rest in him.

When you do, you will discover that Jesus is gentle and lowly in heart. The God of the universe knows and understands and has made himself accessible to you. This is Jesus.

 ## Live It

If you are weary and burdened, accept Jesus' invitation today - come unto him and you'll find rest for your soul.

Day 19 – The Messiah

 ## Hear It

The woman said to him, "I know that Messiah is coming (he who is called Christ). When he comes, he will tell us all things." Jesus said to her, "I who speak to you am he" (John 4:25, 26 ESV).

 ## Believe It

The conversation started with a simple question.

Will you give me a drink?

It ended with a great many people believing that Jesus was and is the Savior of the world.

What happened?

Jesus met a woman who had a dry, thirsty soul. That's what happened.

Jesus knew her story. He knows your story as well.

She had five failed marriages. And the man she was currently with was not her husband. Can you imagine having the details of your life exposed like that? Can you imagine what she was feeling at that moment?

Jesus had already offered her *"living water."* He wasn't exposing the details of her life to condemn her. He also knew exactly who he was and why he had come into the world.

This Samaritan woman gathered her thoughts and said to Jesus, *"I perceive that you must be a prophet."*

Like most Jews and Samaritans, this woman knew the promises of the Old Testament concerning the Messiah. She also knew that when he comes he *"will declare all things to us."*

Jesus said to her, *"I who speak to you am he."* This is why he didn't condemn her. This is why he doesn't condemn you. He is the Messiah, the anointed one, the Christ.

The woman tagged him as a prophet because he knew her story. She discovered that he was so much more.

He is the one who saves us from sin and death, and gives us eternal life. The one who leads us to worship God in spirit and truth.

Now to this Samaritan woman, he offered the one thing that could truly satisfy and refresh her soul – *living water,* water that wells up to eternal life. Water that once you drink you will never be thirsty again. Water that you want to share with others.

And she did. Because she shared her testimony, many came to hear the same life-giving words of Christ. And they found the source of living water for themselves.

 ## Live It

Is your soul thirsty? Have you looked for something to fill the emptiness in your heart? If so, ask Jesus and he will give you a drink that truly satisfies your soul.

And then share the news with others so they, too, will thirst no more.

Day 20 – No Other Name

 ## Hear It

And there is salvation in no one else, for there is no other name under heaven given among men by which we must be saved (Acts 4:12 ESV).

 ## Believe It

God has been telling the world about Jesus since the beginning of time. This story was written down for us through the prophets of old. They foretold over 300 prophecies that Jesus fulfilled. The statistical odds of this happening are staggering.

Those in Israel who were in tune with the story recognized him. A man named Simeon was at the temple when Mary and Joseph brought Jesus there on the eighth day following his birth. Simeon held Jesus in his arms. As he looked at him, Simeon said, *"...my eyes have seen your salvation"* (Luke 2:30).

Years later, Jesus picked disciples to witness his life, his death, his burial, his resurrection and ascension into heaven. They saw Jesus carry out God's plan for the salvation of anyone who would believe in him.

After Jesus ascended into heaven, these men were filled with power from on high. The Holy Spirit emboldened them to lift up the name of Jesus. They did.

Peter was the first to proclaim Jesus to the people. He said, *"This Jesus God raised up, and of that we are all witnesses...God has made him both Lord and Christ, this Jesus whom you crucified"* (Acts 2:32, 36).

When the people heard this they asked what they must do. Peter responded, *"Repent and be baptized...in the name of Jesus Christ for the forgiveness of your sins and you will receive the gift of the Holy Spirit"* (Acts 2:38). Three thousand believed in the name of Jesus that day and were added to the church.

Not long after, Peter and John encountered a lame man at the temple. Peter looked at him and said, *"In the name of Jesus Christ of Nazareth, rise up and walk."* And he did. The people marveled.

This miracle upset the religious leaders. They arrested Peter and John because they "were proclaiming in Jesus the resurrection of the dead." They brought Peter and John out and asked them, "by what power or by what name did you do this?" (Acts 4:7).

Peter, filled with the Spirit, said, *"by the name of Jesus Christ of Nazareth, whom you crucified, whom God raised from the dead—by him this man is standing before you well"* (Acts 4:10).

Jesus is the story. He is the message. The disciples could proclaim no other, because *"there is no other name under heaven given among men by which we must be saved."*

 ## Live It

Someone loved you enough to tell you the story of Jesus. They told you about his death, burial and resurrection. The message cut to the heart and you knew that there was salvation in no other. You believed and were added to the church.

The name of Jesus is now being lifted up through you.

Day 21 – The Man

Hear It

So Jesus said to them, "Truly, truly, I say to you, the Son can do nothing of his own accord, but only what he sees the Father doing. For whatever the Father does, that the Son does likewise (John 5:19 ESV).

Believe It

Jesus is God. He is the one who brought this world into existence. He created everything, and as Colossians 1:17 states, *"in Him, all things hold together."*

Yet, as a man, Jesus lived in dependence on his Father. This is important, because this is the way God designed us to live. We are created beings. The only way to truly flourish is through dependence on our creator.

That really steps on our pride and that fleshly desire to be independent. But that is not the way to genuine joy and true contentment. That is not the way to live life to the full.

Independence is nothing but the lie of the enemy. Adam and Eve bought the lie. In choosing to eat of the tree of the knowledge of good and evil, they declared their independence from God.

The sad story of history is that mankind has tried to make it on its own ever since. All you have to do is watch the evening news to see how that has worked out for us. Our independent, rebellious attitude toward God has made a mess of things.

Thankfully, Jesus showed us the way to truly live as humans. Every situation he faced, every miracle he performed and every truth he taught flowed from this attitude: *"The Son can do nothing by himself."* In the same way, apart from Jesus we *"can do nothing"* (John 15:5).

This dependent life is what Paul had in mind when he wrote, *"Follow my example, as I follow the example of Christ"* (1 Corinthians 11:1). *Jesus humbled himself and became obedient* (Philippians 2:6-8). *He entrusted himself to the one who judges justly* (1 Peter 2:21-23). This was the example Jesus left us to follow. Jesus, the independent one, came to earth, and through his life, showed us how to live in dependence.

We are to trust him, just as he trusted his Father. This is the way for the believer.

 ## Live It

You are a created being. You were created to live in dependence on your creator. When you do, life makes sense. Today, take a lesson from Jesus and declare your dependence on the Son.

Day 22 – The Lamb of God

 ## Hear It

The next day he saw Jesus coming toward him, and said, "Behold, the Lamb of God, who takes away the sin of the world!" (John 1:29 ESV).

 ## Believe It

What if you were tapped as the person who would introduce Jesus to the world…that would identify him as the long awaited Messiah?

Actually, God did tap a person for that job. It was John the Baptist. God sent John to baptize *"that he (Jesus) might be revealed to Israel"* (John 1:31).

You know the story. Jesus went out to the Jordan to be baptized by John. When John lifted Jesus out of the water, the dove descended upon Jesus and a voice came from heaven saying, *"You are my beloved Son. With you I am well pleased."*

Until that moment John did not recognize Jesus as the Messiah. But then he knew.

The next day, John the Baptist saw Jesus. This was his moment, the introduction. It was exactly what needed to be said; *"Behold, the Lamb of God who takes away the sin of the world."*

John's task was done. He introduced Jesus to Israel as the Lamb of God.

This is Jesus…the one who offered himself as the final and complete sacrifice for sin.

Someone introduced Jesus to you. They told you that he died for your sins…that he carried out his role as the Lamb of God on your behalf.

Peter put it this way: *"but with the precious blood of Christ, like that of a lamb without blemish or spot. He was foreknown before the foundation of the world but was made manifest in the last times for the sake of you…"* (1 Peter 1:19, 20).

Aren't you glad someone introduced you to the Lamb of God who took away your sins?

 ## Live It

Jesus is the Lamb of God. This will be our chorus in heaven: *"Worthy is the Lamb that was slain to receive power and riches and wisdom and might and honor and glory and blessing"* (Revelation 5:12 NLT). Let this be the praise of your lips today.

Day 23 – The Son

 ## Hear It

…but these are written so that you may believe that Jesus is the Christ, the Son of God, and that by believing you may have life in his name (John 20:31 ESV).

 ## Believe It

When John set out to write his gospel account, he did so with a clear purpose in mind…"that you may believe that Jesus is the Christ, the Son of God, and that by believing you may have life in his name."

Much of what Jesus did and said didn't make it into John's gospel. He said as much. *"Jesus did many other signs in the presence of his disciples that are not written in this book"* (John 20:30).

He even wrote, *"Were every one of them to be written, I suppose that the world itself could not contain the books that would be written"* (John 21:25).

What John did include, he included to convince you that Jesus was and is exactly who he claimed to be.

- The Word Made Flesh – John 1:1, 14

- The Living Water – John 4:14

- The Messiah – John 4:26

- The Bread of Life – John 6:35

- The Light of the World – John 8:12

- The Great I Am – John 8:58

- The Door – John 10:9

- The Good Shepherd – John 10:11

- The Resurrection and the Life – John 11:25-26

- The Way, the Truth and the Life – John 14:6

- The Vine – John 15:5

- Lord and God – John 20:28

- The Son of God – John 20:31

He did so that you might have eternal life.

 Live it

Have the stories that have been written convinced you that truly Jesus is the Son of God? Have you believed in his name and received eternal life?

This is why John wrote, that you might have life in Jesus's name.

Day 24 – God's Testimony

 ## Hear It

And this is the testimony, that God gave us eternal life, and this life is in his Son. Whoever has the Son has life; whoever does not have the Son of God does not have life. I write these things to you who believe in the name of the Son of God, that you may know that you have eternal life (1 John 5:11-13 ESV).

 ## Believe It

The Bible from beginning to end is God's testimony concerning Jesus.

The testimony is this: God gave us eternal life, and this life is in Jesus.

According to this passage, if you have the Son you have eternal life. If you don't have the Son, you don't have life.

This is the exclusivity of Jesus. He alone has life to give. This is his gift to anyone who believes.

Now the world takes umbrage at God's testimony concerning Jesus. The idea that life is found in Jesus alone is offensive.

It shouldn't be. He is the only one who has overcome the grave, who has rendered death powerless.

All the other religious leaders of world history are still in their graves. And even when they were alive, they didn't claim that eternal life was in them.

You were once dead in trespasses and sins, but now you are alive in Christ. All because you believed God's testimony concerning Jesus and you received his offer of life.

John wrote these clear and powerful words that you may know you eternal life.

Because you have the Son, you have life.

 ## Live It

Christianity is exclusive. It excludes every other religion or philosophy as a means to eternal life. The reason is simple. There is not a person, a place or a philosophy other than Jesus that has life to give. Maybe good advice, or positive affirmations, or practical steps to make the best of life on planet earth, but not eternal life, that living hope that boldly says *"to die is gain"* (Philippians 1:21).

Today, rejoice. You have the Son!

Day 25 – Complete

 ## Hear It

For in him the whole fullness of deity dwells bodily, and you have been filled in him, who is the head of all rule and authority (Colossians 2:9, 10 ESV).

 ## Believe It

The mystery of Jesus, the truth that bends our minds, is that he is both fully God and fully human. Two natures, the divine nature and the human nature, in one body. Theologians call this the *hypostatic* union.

Paul explained it this way: "In him the whole fullness of deity dwells bodily."

Our finite minds will never fully understand this reality. And our feeble attempts to explain how Jesus is both fully God and fully man will fall woefully short. We can, however, learn an important truth from this mystery.

This truth shows that God designed man to live in harmony with him. God and man together.

We see this in creation. God breathed his life into mankind. The first humans enjoyed fellowship with God in the Garden. God with man. Man with God.

We see this in the new creation. That's you. God breathed new life into you through his Spirit. And then he sent his Spirit to dwell in you. God with you. You with God.

This is the way God designed it to be. Now sin and death had their rule over us for a time. Under their reign, we lived alienated from God. Paul described us as *"having no hope and without God in the world"* (Ephesians 2:12).

Jesus

Jesus changed all of that. He brought us near to God through his reconciling work on the cross. He restored harmony. And now we *are being built together into a dwelling of God in the Spirit* (Ephesians 2:22). *"Christ in you, your hope of glory"* (Colossians 1:27).

Jesus is both fully God and fully man. He now lives in you. Which means you are with God and he is with you. And as Paul wrote, you are complete in him, functioning the way God created you to be.

Live It

Jesus is the one who made you whole. In him, you are complete, one with God's Spirit. Live today as a fully functioning human being…God with you, you with God.

Day 26 – Every Knee

Hear It

Therefore God has highly exalted him and bestowed on him the name that is above every name, so that at the name of Jesus every knee should bow, in heaven and on earth and under the earth, and every tongue confess that Jesus Christ is Lord, to the glory of God the Father (Philippians 2:9-11 ESV).

Believe It

We know Jesus Christ as God incarnate. He left his exalted position, humbled himself and became a man. As Paul wrote, *"he emptied himself, by taking the form of a servant, being born in the likeness of men"* (Philippians 2:7).

In this human form, Jesus humbled himself and became obedient to the point of death, the brutal, horrific death he died on a Roman cross. This was his cup to drink. He did so to carry out the will of the Father for you.

He took away your sins once and for all. He redeemed you for his own through his precious blood. That was his work. Before he died, he proclaimed, "It is finished." He completed what God sent him in the world to do.

God highly exalted Jesus and gave him the name that is above every name. You may have "heroes" in your life. People who mentored you, encouraged you, helped you find your life's purpose. Their names are precious to you. But none have a name like Jesus. You would never call on them for salvation.

That name is Jesus. *"Everyone who calls upon the name of the Lord shall be saved"* (Romans 10:13). His is the name above every other.

One day every knee will bow, and every tongue will confess that Jesus Christ is Lord. Aren't you glad that day has already come for you…the day that you in humble faith, bowed the knee of your heart to the risen Christ and confessed with your mouth that Jesus Christ is Lord?

Live It

Much of the world is in the dark concerning the true nature of Jesus. That was true when he lived on planet earth. It is true today. Just who is this Jesus really? Sadly, the world slots him as one name among many religious leaders. It puts him on par with Confucius, Buddha, and Mohammed.

You know the truth. He is not one among many. He is the Lord Jesus Christ. His name is above every other, because salvation is in no other.

Rejoice, you know the real Jesus. You know him as Lord, as Savior, as life. You have the joy of making his name known in the world.

Day 27 – The Transfiguration

 ## Hear It

And he was transfigured before them, and his face shone like the sun, and his clothes became white as light (Matthew 17:2 ESV).

 ## Believe It

Moses asked a very bold question of God. *"Please, show me your glory"* (Exodus 33:18).

No one had ever seen God face to face. Man would not be able to survive the sheer power of God's being and glory. But God did pass by Moses, but only after he hid him in the cleft of a rock, and covered Moses with his hand. Once he passed by, God removed his hand. Moses caught a glimpse of God's "back."

This glimpse radiated Moses' face. Moses was unaware, but when he came down from the mountain, the people were afraid to get near him. Moses kept a veil over his face.

The point is that God revealed himself to Moses. Peter, James and John had a similar experience.

It happened after Jesus asked them this question; *"Who do you say that I am?"* Peter answered, *"You are the Christ, the Son of the living God."* Jesus took Peter, James and John with him to the top of a mountain.

Jesus was transfigured right before their eyes. His face shone like the sun, and his clothes became white as light.

Moses and Elijah appeared to them as well. This is fascinating. The one who asked God to show him his glory was there to see the glory of God in the face of Jesus Christ.

Peter, impetuous Peter, started to speak. But as he did, God's voice overpowered the scene: *"This is my beloved Son, with whom I am well pleased; listen to him"* (Matthew 17:5).

Peter, James and John saw the glory of Jesus. That moment erased any doubt they had about Jesus's identity.

You've seen the glory of God in the face of Jesus Christ. At that moment, you learned that he is the Lord, the one who is merciful and gracious, and steadfast in his love for you.

 ## Live It

One day you will see Christ in all of his glory. When he is revealed, you also will be revealed with him in glory.

For now, rejoice in this wonderful truth: *"And we all, with unveiled face, beholding the glory of the Lord, are being transformed into the same image from one degree of glory to another. For this comes from the Lord who is the Spirit"* (2 Corinthians 3:18).

Day 28 – Focused

Hear It

Therefore, since we are surrounded by so great a cloud of witnesses, let us also lay aside every weight, and sin which clings so closely, and let us run with endurance the race that is set before us, looking to Jesus, the founder and perfecter of our faith, who for the joy that was set before him endured the cross, despising the shame, and is seated at the right hand of the throne of God (Hebrews 12:1, 2 ESV).

Believe It

Faith is the Christian's way of life. It's how we believers live day in and day out.

We weren't always believers. We came into the world lost and dead in sin. We were sinners by nature. We followed the ways of the world and lived to gratify the desires of the flesh.

A day came when we met Jesus. He turned our hearts from unbelief to belief in him. That's faith. He brought it about. He was the author, or the originator, of faith in us.

Paul explained this in his letter to the church in Rome. *"Faith comes from hearing, and hearing through the word of Christ"* (Romans 10:17).

Jesus is the substance or essence of faith. Our faith is in him. This is important to understand. Many believers think of faith as a power in and of itself. That's not true. There is no faith apart from him. We live by faith in the Son of God (Galatians 2:20).

Jesus is our focus. The writer of Hebrews calls each of us to run the race set before us with our eyes fully fixed on Jesus. In the same way he authored faith in us at salvation, he will perfect it in us as we run with endurance.

This is true in every circumstance of life, including our trials and tribulations.

Look at what Jesus does through our sufferings: *"Not only that, but we rejoice in our sufferings, knowing that suffering produces endurance, and endurance produces character, and character produces hope, and hope does not put us to shame, because God's love has been poured into our hearts through the Holy Spirit who has been given to us"* (Romans 5:3-5).

And through our trials: *"...so that the tested genuineness of your faith—more precious than gold that perishes though it is tested by fire—may be found to result in praise and glory and honor at the revelation of Jesus Christ"* (1 Peter 1:7).

When we keep our eyes on Jesus, we see time and time again that he is faithful to us. We see through every circumstance that he is enough.

It's no wonder the writer of Hebrews tells us to keep our eyes focused on him.

 ## Live It

When it comes to faith, Jesus made it clear that the size of our faith doesn't matter. Faith the size of a mustard seed can move mountains. Why, because it is the object of our faith that matters. His name is Jesus.

Maybe you've prayed for more faith, or more effective faith. If so, will you change your prayer? Ask God to keep your eyes focused on Jesus, focused on his power and might, his majesty, his love and grace. He will take care of your faith. Just as he originated it in you, he will bring it to maturity by showing you his faithfulness.

Day 29 – Knowing God

Hear It

And this is eternal life, that they know you, the only true God, and Jesus Christ whom you have sent (John 17:3 ESV).

Believe It

How would you define eternal life? If you have ever wondered, John 17:3 provides the answer. Short and simple, eternal life is knowing God and knowing Jesus. This is not merely head knowledge. It's relational knowledge experienced in the heart; knowledge that is personal and intimate.

This eternal life is the promise of the New Covenant–*"for they shall all know me, from the least of them to the greatest"* (Hebrews 8:11). Dan DeHaan, a wonderful bible teacher, wrote, *"God created men to know Him. God created men to enjoy Him."* Jesus, through his death and resurrection, opened the way for this to be a possibility not just in the by and by, but here and now.

God took away your sins, reconciled you to himself, justified you, sanctified you, made you alive, and poured his Spirit into your life for this single purpose. It is a *"by grace through faith"* relationship, a spiritual union that conforms us to the likeness of Jesus. In other words, God rubs off on us, and we become like him.

Many years ago a friend died of cancer. The last time I saw him he was standing before a crowd at a church youth camp sharing his story. Although he talked about the cancer, his story was John 17:3. As I watched and listened to him that day, I saw a young man who genuinely knew the Lord, who was experiencing eternal life.

This deep personal relationship he enjoyed with Jesus changed him. He had come to know Jesus and there was nothing better in life. He had taken hold of eternal life and everyday was one more opportunity to grow in his knowledge of Christ Jesus.

Jesus Christ died and was raised so that we could know God. And knowing him changes us. That is what my friend discovered.

 Live It

Rejoice. In Christ, you know the God of the universe. Even more amazing, the God of the universe knows you and loves you. As Jesus said, this is eternal life.

Day 30 – The Prize

Hear It

But whatever gain I had, I counted as loss for the sake of Christ. Indeed, I count everything as loss because of the surpassing worth of knowing Christ Jesus my Lord. For his sake I have suffered the loss of all things and count them as rubbish, in order that I may gain Christ (Philippians 3:7, 8).

Believe It

Paul had much to brag about as a human being.

He was from the right pedigree. He was educated by the best. He was a leader and a rising star among the Pharisees. He was zealous for his way of life, all in. And according to the righteousness in the law, he was found blameless.

Very few in Israel could compete with this resume. For Paul, these things defined him. This is where he derived his identity and found his purpose.

He was deeply entrenched in the Jewish way of life. When Christianity posed a threat, he took action to get rid of this new sect. As he wrote in Philippians, he was *"a persecutor of the church."*

That was his intent in his journey to Damascus. He was equipped with papers authorizing him to arrest any Jew belonging to the Way and bring them to Jerusalem to stand trial before the chief priests.

When he arrived in Damascus, he was a changed man. Instead of arresting Christians, he proclaimed in the synagogues that Jesus *"is the Son of God."*

What happened? Paul met Jesus. He learned the truth about Jesus, truth that set him free.

Jesus set Paul apart as one of his chosen instruments *"to bear My name before the Gentiles and kings and the sons of Israel"* (Acts 9:15).

At that moment everything changed.

All that Paul deemed important became nothing more than rubbish compared to the surpassing worth of knowing Christ. He lived for this purpose: *"that I may know him."*

This became his driving ambition, his singular goal. As he wrote, *"for me to live is Christ."*

 Live It

Christianity is not a religion. Christianity is Jesus Christ. You have the joy and privilege of knowing him and walking in his love. You have the privilege of making him known in this world of darkness

God has and is revealing himself to you in the person and work of Jesus Christ. Adopt Paul's philosophy—that I may know him—as your philosophy. There is no greater adventure in life than growing in your knowledge of Jesus Christ. Everything else is merely rubbish compared to the surpassing worth of knowing him who is your life.

Jesus

Dear Reader,

I pray this devotional has deepened your understanding of Jesus Christ. Knowing Jesus is the adventure of a lifetime!

I would love to stay in contact with you. Please feel free to reach out to me at bob@basicgospel.net. I also invite you to join me each weekday for *Basic Gospel*, either on your local station (basicgospel.net/stations) or at Facebook.com/basicgospel or YouTube.com/basicgospel.

In Him,

Bob Christopher
@rcchristopherjr

Scan the QR code for quick access.

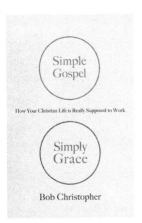

"We're all natural-born legalists," says Bob Christopher. "We try to live for God, but it's impossible to do."

Why? Because all our efforts and ideas are based on the same fear-based, guilt-driven plot line: Try harder. As you've undoubtedly noticed, it just doesn't work.

Simple Gospel, Simply Grace showcases an alternative, which is actually God's original plan: Everything you're trying to achieve in the Christian life has already been given to you—from God, by grace, in Christ.

Do you struggle to receive what God has freely given? How can you begin to experience true freedom, assurance of your forgiveness, and victory over sin? How can the power that raised Jesus from the dead enable you to live and love the way He did?

You'll discover the answers in this crystal-clear portrayal of the simple gospel—which is simply grace.

Get your copy today!
simplegospelsimplygrace.com
or 844.412.2742

Made in the USA
Monee, IL
21 January 2021

To D████y
love Hannah

Christmas
2005

Daddy

PRESENTED TO

Hannah

PRESENTED BY

12-25-05

DATE

PROVERBS FOR LIFE™

for Dads

Ⴘ

inspirio™

Proverbs for Life ™ for Dads
ISBN 0-310-80190-7

Copyright © 2004 by GRQ Ink, Inc.
Franklin, Tennessee 37067
"Proverbs for Life" is a trademark owned by GRQ, Inc.

Published by Inspirio™, The gift group of Zondervan
5300 Patterson Avenue, SE
Grand Rapids, Michigan 49530

Requests for information should be addressed to:
Inspirio™, The gift group of Zondervan
Grand Rapids, Michigan 49530
http://www.inspiriogifts.com

Compiler: Lila Empson
Associate Editor: Janice Jacobson
Project Manager: Tom Dean
Manuscript written by Ed Strauss in conjunction with
    Snapdragon Editorial Group, Inc.
Design: Whisner Design Group

Printed in China.

03 04 05/HK/ 4 3 2 1

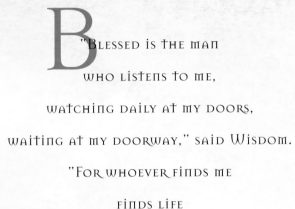

B"Blessed is the man

who listens to me,

watching daily at my doors,

waiting at my doorway," said Wisdom.

"For whoever finds me

finds life

and receives favor

from the Lord."

Proverbs 8:34–35 niv

Contents

Introduction

The book of Proverbs contains the timeless wisdom each person needs to live a happy, healthy, well-balanced life—each entry teaching a practical principle designed to encourage good choices and positive problem solving.

Proverbs for Life™ for Dads takes those valuable principles and applies them to the issues you care about most—such as family, health, peace, and commitment. As you read through these pages, may you find the practical answers—God's answers—to the questions you are asking.

The prayer of the upright pleases the LORD.

— Proverbs 15:8 NIV

The Praying Dad

The only crown I ask

dear Lord, to wear

Is this—that I may teach a little child,

I do not ask that I should ever stand

Among the wise, the worthy, or the great;

I only ask that softly, hand in hand,

A child and I may enter at your gate.

Saint Ignatius of Loyola

Your Children Are Watching

Teach children how they should live, and they will remember it all their life.

— *Proverbs 22:6 GNT*

No matter who you are or what kind of life you are living, your children are watching you. Whether you are talking to a telephone solicitor, coping with the household budget, driving in rush-hour traffic, or taking out the trash, they're watching you. They are learning, following, and trying to be just like you. You will want to set an example that will point them to God.

Abraham set that kind of example for his son Isaac by demonstrating obedience to God and unswerving faith throughout his life. So great was his righteousness that it stands even today as a standard for faith and godliness. His living example affected not only the life of Isaac but also the lives of Abraham's sons and daughters for countless and continuing generations.

Resolve for your children to be the best example of godly faith and steadfast commitment possible. Know that as you keep your eyes focused on God, they, too, will keep their eyes focused on their living example—you.

Raising your children is a great privilege and responsibility. Ask God to help you be a living example of godliness and faith by helping you see the strengths and weaknesses in your words, attitudes, and actions. Then go to work shoring up the weak areas. Find someone—a trusted friend—who will encourage you and keep you on track by providing encouragement and accountability. As you direct your footsteps to God, be sure that your children will be walking in your footsteps straight to God.

TRY THIS: *Make a list of character traits, such as honesty, courage, compassion, holiness. Look up scriptures for each trait in the topical index of a study Bible. Ask God to give you opportunities to demonstrate that trait as an example to your children. At the beginning of each week, move to the next trait on the list.*

THE RIGHTEOUS MAN LEADS A BLAMELESS LIFE; BLESSED ARE HIS CHILDREN AFTER HIM.

PROVERBS 20:7 NIV

IN ALL THINGS YOU YOURSELF MUST BE AN EXAMPLE OF GOOD BEHAVIOR.

TITUS 2:7 GNT

He that gives good advice builds with one hand; he that gives good counsel and example builds with both.

FRANCIS BACON

Standing by the Truth

Do not let kindness and truth leave you.

— *Proverbs 3:3 NASB*

An honest man's the noblest work of God.

Alexander Pope

Daniel looked at the disappointed faces of his three children around the dinner table. Just yesterday, they had been looking forward to a day at Splash World on Friday, but today everything had changed. When he asked for the day off, Daniel's boss said no. No explanation, no discussion, just no.

Daniel was a little annoyed by his boss's response. A few weeks earlier the same thing had happened to one of his coworkers. But when the boss told her no, she just called in sick and took the day off anyway. The boss never seemed to have noticed.

It would have been easy to follow his coworker's example. It sure seemed better than disappointing his kids, who didn't understand why their plans had to change. But Daniel knew what kind of father he would be if he taught his children to be honest and didn't hold himself to the same standard. He'd just have to find a way to make it up to them.

Setting a standard of honesty for your children means setting the same standard for yourself. Even if they never know about a dishonest act, you will. That seed of dishonesty will steal your resolve, your confidence, and your conviction every time you have to deal with the issue of honesty in your children's lives. Don't put yourself at a disadvantage. Keep your commitment to honesty strong and constant—for your children's sake as well as for your own.

Try this: Prepare a small card for your wallet that reads, "With God's help and for the sake of my children (name your children here) _____, _____, _____, I will be truthful and honest at all times in word and deed." Put this in one of the windows in your wallet or on the bathroom mirror where you will see it often.

You will know the truth, and the truth will set you free.

John 8:32 NIV

Buy the truth and do not sell it; get wisdom, discipline and understanding.

Proverbs 23:23 NIV

I hope I shall possess firmness and virtue enough to maintain what I consider the most enviable of all titles, the character of an honest man.

George Washington

13

THE HAPPY DAD

For memories of childhood days
And all that you have done
To make our home a happy place
And growing up such fun.

You made my world a better place
And through the coming years,
I'll keep these memories of you
As cherished souvenirs!

Author Unknown

Blessed is he who trusts in the LORD.

~ *Proverbs* 16:20 NIV

My children, listen to me: happy are those who keep my ways.

~ *Proverbs* 8:32 NRSV

To be happy at home is the ultimate result of all ambition.

Samuel Johnson

Paying the Bill

To do what is right and just is more acceptable to the Lord than sacrifice.

~ *Proverbs 21:3 NIV*

Gary couldn't believe his eyes when his son Steve's golf ball hit a tree near the seventeenth hole, bounced into the street, and smashed the headlight of a passing car. It happened so fast that the driver didn't even realize it had happened and kept going. Gary and Steve yelled and waved until the driver stopped a few yards down the street. They explained what had happened to the surprised driver and offered to replace the headlight. A few days later, the driver delivered a bill for $278, far more than they had imagined.

"Dad, do I have to pay it?" Steve asked. "It was an accident, and that man wouldn't even have known if we hadn't told him. It will take me forever to save that much money."

"That's true," Gary responded. "But accident or not, your ball caused the damage. Taking responsibility is the right thing to do, even if it costs more than we expected. We'll pay this bill together."

Your children need to know that failing to take responsibility for their actions—intentional or otherwise—will affect every relationship they have. Unless you teach them to acknowledge their mistakes, they won't learn about God's forgiveness. And unless they have been taught to own up to their mistakes and make restitution, they will grow insensitive in their relationships with others. Gary was a wise father. He realized that $278 was a small price to pay for such an important lesson.

Try this: *The next time someone calls into question your child's conduct—a hurtful remark, a traffic ticket, an accidental collision at poolside—take time to be sure that he or she acknowledges his or her responsibility in the incident and works out a plan to make it right.*

RIGHTEOUS PEOPLE ARE SURE OF THEMSELVES.

PROVERBS 21:29 GNT

A WISE MAN'S HEART GUIDES HIS MOUTH, AND HIS LIPS PROMOTE INSTRUCTION.

PROVERBS 16:23 NIV

The most important thought I ever had was that of my individual responsibility to God.

DANIEL WEBSTER

17

I'll Always Be There

A friend loves at all times.

~ *Proverbs 17:17 NASB*

It's important that your children know that you love them deeply, and that you're not going to stop loving them no matter what they do. They need to know that they can rely on you to love them always, that you'll always be available to them when they need you.

The Prodigal Son knew that his father loved him. Even when he felt unworthy of the close father-son relationship he once enjoyed, he knew that if he went to his father for help he wouldn't be turned away. His father had always shown him love, kindness and caring, and had always provided for his needs. As it turned out, he discovered that his father loved him deeply and unconditionally.

You don't want your kids to misbehave or get in trouble, but they sometimes will. If they know that you love them deeply, they'll know they can come to you during those times.

When you make a commitment to your children, it doesn't automatically mean that you'll be able to give them all the time that you'd like to. Spending quality time with your children is important, as is attending events they're involved in. Being committed to your children goes deeper still. Assure your children that you will always be on their side and available to help them when they need you the most, no matter what.

TRY THIS: *Next time your child goes through a personal crisis, remind your child of your love with a note. For boys: "I am your father. I will always love you." For girls, buy a rose, snip off the thorns, and write: "I'll always be there for you."*

"I WILL NOT TAKE MY LOVE FROM HIM, NOR WILL I EVER BETRAY MY FAITHFULNESS," SAYS THE LORD.

PSALM 89:33 NIV

"I WILL ALWAYS BE WITH YOU; I WILL NEVER ABANDON YOU," SAYS THE LORD.

JOSHUA 1:5 GNT

The parent-adolescent relationship is like a partnership in which the senior partner (the parent) has more expertise in many areas but looks forward to the day when the junior partner (the adolescent) will take over the business of running his or her own life.

LAURENCE STEINBERG

They're Not Born with It

Sensible people will see trouble coming and avoid it.

~ *Proverbs* 22:3 GNT

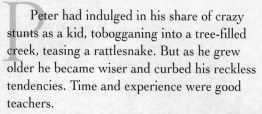

Peter had indulged in his share of crazy stunts as a kid, tobogganing into a tree-filled creek, teasing a rattlesnake. But as he grew older he became wiser and curbed his reckless tendencies. Time and experience were good teachers.

Yet when his son Tommy fell off a gate and banged his skull on the stone pathway, and by a miracle received only a bruise, Peter's first thought was, *Why was he sitting on a wobbly gate? Doesn't he know it's dangerous?*

Apparently Tommy didn't know, not before he climbed up, anyway. Tommy probably wouldn't climb up on the same gate again very soon. But Peter knew there were plenty of other dangerous stunts that Tommy would try before he was old enough to know better. As Peter held an ice cube on his son's bump, he remembered the lessons he'd learned as a child and decided it was time to share one of his foolish mistakes with Tommy.

According to Job, ostriches missed out when God was passing out common sense. The difference between kids and ostriches is that although kids aren't born with a lot of good sense, given time, experience, and a few accidents, they will acquire it. Make your child's learning experience as painless as possible by helping him or her to recognize potential danger. When your children were toddlers you childproofed the house. When they're older, teach them how to recognize and avoid danger.

Try this: During family time tell your children stories about some of the reckless things you did as a child and how you paid for your foolishness. If your parents warned you something was dangerous but you did it anyway and suffered as a result, stress that lesson. Your kids will enjoy the stories.

WHEN I WAS A CHILD, I TALKED LIKE A CHILD, I THOUGHT LIKE A CHILD, I REASONED LIKE A CHILD. WHEN I BECAME A MAN, I PUT CHILDISH WAYS BEHIND ME.

I CORINTHIANS 13:11 NIV

A WISE SON HEEDS HIS FATHER'S INSTRUCTION.

PROVERBS 13:1 NIV

In our childhood we survived reckless danger and became wiser. May our experiences serve to spare our children from running the same gauntlet.

KENNETH P. WALTERS

It Hurts Me More

Discipline your children and you can always be proud of them.

— Proverbs 29:17 GNT

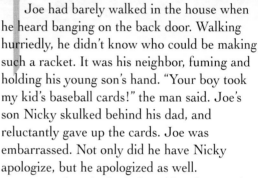

Joe had barely walked in the house when he heard banging on the back door. Walking hurriedly, he didn't know who could be making such a racket. It was his neighbor, fuming and holding his young son's hand. "Your boy took my kid's baseball cards!" the man said. Joe's son Nicky skulked behind his dad, and reluctantly gave up the cards. Joe was embarrassed. Not only did he have Nicky apologize, but he apologized as well.

Joe and Nicky had planned on leaving for an afternoon of fishing, but Joe knew that he couldn't ignore this incident. With a heavy heart, he took his son aside to talk with him about his behavior and to inform him that the fishing trip was off.

Nicky knew that his dad loved fishing and had been looking forward to the time together. By calling off the trip, Joe was not only punishing his son but was sharing his son's punishment. Nicky realized this was serious but that his dad cared.

✺ A dad needs to discipline children for the same reason that God disciplines dads—because he loves and cares for them, and because he knows that bad behavior hurts the perpetrator and others. The word translated *discipline* in the Bible usually means "to instruct, train up," and that's God's purpose for discipline—to teach us how to live better and how to live closer to him. Those motives are likewise a dad's.

✺ TRY THIS: *To remind yourself that the purpose for discipline is to instruct and teach, keep a small piece of chalk in your change tray. Every time you need to discipline one of your children, pick up the chalk and let it remind you that the purpose of discipline is to write a lesson on your child's heart.*

O LORD, DO NOT REBUKE ME IN YOUR ANGER OR DISCIPLINE ME IN YOUR WRATH.

PSALM 6:1 NIV

HE WHO SPARES THE ROD HATES HIS SON, BUT HE WHO LOVES HIM IS CAREFUL TO DISCIPLINE HIM.

PROVERBS 13:24 NIV

To make punishments efficacious, two things are necessary; they must never be disproportional to the offence, and they must be certain.

WILLIAM G. SIMMS

23

The Understanding Dad

I've seen my children make a mess
Where messes shouldn't be,
I've seen them slow to come when called
Although I've counted "three."

But God has patience with mere men,
He knows we are but dust,
And so I say, "My kids are kids,
They'll grow in God, I trust."

Ed Strauss

Whoever is slow to anger has great understanding.

~ *Proverbs* 14:29 NRSV

As a father is kind to his children, so the LORD is kind to those who honor him.

~ *Psalm* 103:13 GNT

ALL, EVERYTHING THAT I UNDERSTAND, I UNDERSTAND ONLY BECAUSE I LOVE.

LEO TOLSTOY

Best-Laid Plans

Commit your work to the LORD, and your plans will be established.

~ *Proverbs* 16:3 *NRSV*

Man proposes
but God
disposes.

Thomas à Kempis

Tom never had a tree house when he was a boy, but he had always wanted one. When his kids came up with the idea to build one in the big oak tree in their backyard, his old dream again caught fire. He envisioned a layout as grandiose as something out of a Tarzan movie.

After drawing some sketches and getting an idea of what materials would cost, Tom realized it was more than his budget and busy schedule could manage. Tom shared the dilemma with his wife, and they discussed several possible options. But they rejected each possibility; none seemed feasible. Finally Tom and his wife decided to pray for God's direction and help.

A week later Tom's younger brother, Chuck, came to live with them for two months. Not only was Chuck a professional carpenter, but he insisted on paying something for room and board. By the time Chuck moved out, the tree house was a reality.

It's important to make plans to avoid drifting from one unfinished project to another. It's even more important, however, to recognize that God is infinitely more far-sighted than you are and knows all things. He knows what will work out and what won't. Even when you can accomplish something on your own, enlisting God as your partner will make the process go more smoothly. Don't hesitate to include God in your plans, and trust him to provide what's needed for a successful outcome.

Try this: Get in the habit of carrying a kernel of popcorn in your pocket. Every time you see that kernel, let it remind you that you're down in the corn maze, but God is up above; he has the big picture and knows what you should do. All you need to do is pray and ask him.

IF THE LORD DOES NOT BUILD THE HOUSE, THE WORK OF THE BUILDERS IS USELESS.

PSALM 127:1 GNT

DELIGHT YOURSELF IN THE LORD AND HE WILL GIVE YOU THE DESIRES OF YOUR HEART.

PSALM 37:4 NIV

Trust in God does not supersede the employment of prudent means on our part.

PASQUIER QUESNEL

27

OUR FATHER

The LORD hears the prayer of the righteous.

~ *Proverbs 15:29* NASB

Greg loved God with all his heart, and he did all he could to live in a way that was pleasing to him. Nevertheless, he felt uncomfortable praying for his own needs. He simply felt he was unworthy to ask God for anything and that his needs were too petty for God's attention. Then one day he overheard his daughter, Brittany, talking to her friend.

"Why don't you just ask your dad for it?" Liz asked.

"No," Brittany replied glumly. "I blew it last week. I don't think he'd want to do anything for me right now."

There was silence for a moment, then Liz said, "Well, yeah . . . but he's your dad, right? You're still his daughter, right? Just ask him."

Greg realized that his love for his daughter gave her the courage to approach him, so God's love for him should give him that same confidence. As a child of his heavenly Father, God would hear and answer his prayers.

❧ Your personal concept of God's nature—whether you view him as a forgiving Father or a harsh, demanding disciplinarian—affects whether you have confidence that he loves you. This in turn determines whether you believe that he hears and cares about your prayers. While it's true that God does not like sin, he also freely forgives. You can be confident to ask him for help when you need it.

❧ TRY THIS: *Every time you look in the mirror and shave, remind yourself that your relationship with God is a result of Jesus' death on the cross, and that you are the child of your Father in heaven. You might even want to hang a small cross on your mirror to help you keep the right perspective.*

THE SPIRIT MAKES YOU GOD'S CHILDREN, AND BY THE SPIRIT'S POWER WE CRY OUT TO GOD, "FATHER! MY FATHER!"

ROMANS 8:15 GNT

JESUS SAID, "HOW MUCH MORE WILL YOUR FATHER IN HEAVEN GIVE GOOD GIFTS TO THOSE WHO ASK HIM!"

MATTHEW 7:11 NIV

The more a man bows his knee before God, the straighter he stands before men.

AUTHOR UNKNOWN

Let It Go

He who covers over an offense promotes love.

~ *Proverbs 17:9* NIV

Steve was lying on his back trying to fix the kitchen sink. From the living room he heard his two daughters quarreling. Their argument grew louder and louder until they came running into the kitchen in tears, the youngest wailing, "She's calling me names!"

Steve scooted out from under the sink and reached out to his daughters. He asked each one to tell her side of the story. Finally he persuaded his older daughter to apologize. He then asked his younger daughter, "There. Now do you forgive your sister?" The younger daughter refused. "God says we should forgive others," Steve reminded her.

"I know it's hard to forgive sometimes," Steve said. "Remember last year when that man said all those bad things about me, and refused to pay the money he owed? His words really hurt. At first it was hard to forgive. But I forgave him."

Steve's daughter nodded thoughtfully. "Okay, I forgive her," she said.

30

❧ You teach your children not only by your words, but by your example. Sometimes you tell them that they need to forgive each other and let wrongs go—yet you also have difficulty forgiving others. Perhaps you feel that the wrongs children suffer are small compared to the more serious affronts you suffer as an adult. But you need to forgive as well, not only for your own spiritual health, but to be an example of godly love, forgiveness, and restitution to your children.

❧ TRY THIS: *If you are having difficulty letting an offense go, make it a matter of prayer every day. When you have forgiven the one who hurt you, share that testimony with your children. You don't need to tell them names and specific details, but they will greatly benefit from your example of forgiveness.*

FORGIVE US OUR SINS, AS WE ALSO FORGIVE EVERYONE WHO SINS AGAINST US.

LUKE 11:4 NIRV

YOU MUST FORGIVE ONE ANOTHER JUST AS THE LORD HAS FORGIVEN YOU. AND TO ALL THESE QUALITIES ADD LOVE.

COLOSSIANS 3:13 GNT

Never does the human soul appear so strong and noble as when it foregoes revenge and dares to forgive an injury.

EDWIN H. CHAPIN

Savings Plan

Ants are creatures of little strength, yet they store up their food in the summer.

~ *Proverbs* 30:25 NIV

Fabulously rich Solomon learned about saving from ants. We can too.

Author Unknown.

A battered blue van drove down the tree-lined road that wound through the grounds of State University. Gilbert had worked hard to make this day possible, and he now was proud to be driving his son there. The back of the van was full of Duane's suitcases, books, and dormitory furnishings.

Duane looked over at his dad. Gilbert had earned his living as a mechanic, his hands were callused and permanently stained with oil. Gilbert beamed. Duane grinned and shook his head. "Dad, I don't understand how you were able to save money for my college education. We never had money to spare. How did you do it?"

Gilbert laughed. "King Solomon said, 'Go study the ant.' So I did. Ants not only know they need to prepare for the future, but they reach that goal by keeping at it consistently, day after day, one grain at a time. I started early, kept at it, and reached my goal. Now you can too."

As a father, you know that you have a responsibility to provide for your children. You probably take that responsibility seriously. You wouldn't dream of seeing your kids do without their basic needs. But in today's world, providing for your children also means preparing now for future needs. That includes setting aside money for their higher education. If you save money faithfully, month after month, year after year, it will add up, especially if you start early and let compound interest start working.

Try this: *Discuss the need for an education fund with your wife and start one this week. Decide what you can afford and faithfully put funds into it. If you aren't able to start a savings account, buy yourself a change bank and put your change in it each day. When it's full, open that account and let your change feed it regularly.*

CHILDREN ARE NOT RESPONSIBLE TO SAVE UP FOR THEIR PARENTS, BUT PARENTS FOR THEIR CHILDREN.

2 CORINTHIANS 12:14 NASB

HE WHO GATHERS MONEY LITTLE BY LITTLE MAKES IT GROW.

PROVERBS 13:11 NIV

Every good father provides for his children's present needs; it is a prudent and industrious father who provides for their future needs.

CHARLES W. FOXE

The Honorable Dad

I'll always remember my father:
He was as honest as the day is long.
His life was marked by integrity,
And his sense of honor—strong.

He was true to his wife and family,
He admitted when he was mistaken.
He was fair and kind; he slurred no man,
My respect for him stands unshaken.

ED STRAUSS

The hope of the righteous is gladness.

~ *Proverbs* 10:28 NASB

If a man therefore purge himself from [dishonorable teachers], he shall be a vessel unto honour.

~ *2 Timothy* 2:21 KJV

LIFE EVERY MAN HOLDS DEAR; BUT THE DEAR MAN HOLDS HONOR FAR MORE PRECIOUS THAN LIFE.

WILLIAM SHAKESPEARE

Stand Tall

Those who do what is right are as bold as lions.

~ Proverbs 28:1 NIrV

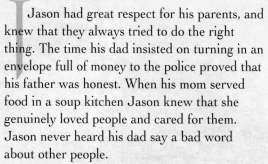

MY STRENGTH IS
AS THE STRENGTH
OF TEN, BECAUSE
MY HEART IS
PURE.

ALFRED, LORD
TENNYSON

Jason had great respect for his parents, and knew that they always tried to do the right thing. The time his dad insisted on turning in an envelope full of money to the police proved that his father was honest. When his mom served food in a soup kitchen Jason knew that she genuinely loved people and cared for them. Jason never heard his dad say a bad word about other people.

One day Jason was hanging out with some friends, just talking about life in general, when Landon, the toughest and supposedly coolest boy, said, "My dad says Christians act righteous, but they're the worst for cheating you."

Up until that point, Jason had been in awe of Landon, but now Jason stood up to him. It was clear just how wrong Landon was. He refuted him so boldly that Landon was left speechless. Jason told story after story about things his parents had done.

If you want your children to take ownership of their faith, let your life be an example to them of what Christianity is about. If you want them to be sold out in their faith, be passionate about yours. It means that if you're doing your best to obey the truth, that dedication will give you boldness and power. Your example is bound to rub off on your children.

Try this: *Any time you're tempted to lie, take advantage of someone in a business deal or compromise your Christian faith in any way, look at a picture of your children and tell yourself, "For their sakes I will stand tall. I will not do anything that weakens my children's confidence in me and in God."*

How blessed is everyone who fears the Lord, who walks in His ways.

Psalm 128:1 NASB

If our hearts do not condemn us, we have confidence before God and receive from Him anything we ask, because we obey His commands and do what pleases Him.

1 John 3:21–22 NIV

The men who succeed best in public life are those who take the risk of standing by their own conviction.

James A. Garfield

Becoming a Better Dad

A wise man will hear and increase in learning, and a man of understanding will acquire wise counsel.

~ *Proverbs 1:5 NASB*

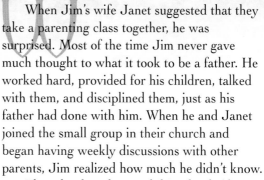

The end of learning is to know God, and out of that knowledge to love Him, and to imitate Him.

John Milton

When Jim's wife Janet suggested that they take a parenting class together, he was surprised. Most of the time Jim never gave much thought to what it took to be a father. He worked hard, provided for his children, talked with them, and disciplined them, just as his father had done with him. When he and Janet joined the small group in their church and began having weekly discussions with other parents, Jim realized how much he didn't know.

Then the thought struck him that he'd never stay current in his career if he approached his job with the same mind-set. Yet being a father was a much more important responsibility with longer-lasting consequences.

When the class ended, Jim's enjoyed his newfound confidence in his parenting skills. He was astounded by how much he'd learned in such a short time. Still, he realized that he would need more instruction and a lot more help from God in the future.

Most parents feel they could use some help raising their children. It is, after all, the greatest challenge, the greatest responsibility, the greatest joy any adult could face. And the irony is that little parenting instruction is offered in the course of a formal education. But help is available. Churches and community colleges, as well as government-sponsored programs, often offer classes. Do all you can to become the parent God intends you to be.

TRY THIS: *What new parenting tip have you learned recently? Write it out on a card, date it, and place it in your Bible. Do the same with each new insight you receive—whether it comes from your own experience, a book, or another parent's wise counsel. Once a month, go through the cards and review what you have learned.*

TEACH ME WHAT I CANNOT SEE; IF I HAVE DONE WRONG, I WILL NOT DO SO AGAIN.

JOB 34:32 NIV

PARENTS, DO NOT TREAT YOUR CHILDREN IN SUCH A WAY AS TO MAKE THEM ANGRY. INSTEAD RAISE THEM WITH CHRISTIAN DISCIPLINE AND INSTRUCTION.

EPHESIANS 6:4 GNT

We learn as much from our children as they learn from us.

AMERICAN PROVERB

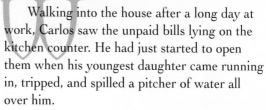

Smile Lines

A merry heart maketh a cheerful countenance.

~ *Proverbs* 15:13 KJV

GOOD HUMOR
IS THE HEALTH
OF THE SOUL;
SADNESS IS ITS
POISON.

LESZINSKY
STANISLAUS

Walking into the house after a long day at work, Carlos saw the unpaid bills lying on the kitchen counter. He had just started to open them when his youngest daughter came running in, tripped, and spilled a pitcher of water all over him.

Carlos stood there incredulous, and then he burst in laughter. Dabbing at his clothes and the bills with a dishtowel, he said, "I guess God knew I needed a bath!" His other kids walked in just then and shook with laughter at the sight.

As Carlos went off to his room to shower and change, he whispered a prayer of thanks to God. His wife's illness and hospitalization, the ever-increasing stack of medical bills, and the care of his four children had taken a toll on him. But he was thankful that he could still enjoy so many moments of humor—God's gift to lighten his heart and the hearts of his kids.

Researchers say that laughing is great for your health. It reduces stress by reducing hormones released during the stress response. It also increases your tolerance to pain and releases infection-fighting antibodies. What's more, humor increases your attentiveness, your heart rate, and even your energy level—meaning you'll get more work done if you laugh. If you can look on the funny side of things, you'll not only be happier, but healthier and more productive—maybe even a better dad.

Try this: Add some humor to your everyday life by checking out a book of jokes from the library and memorizing a few of the best ones. Make a point of repeating them to your children each day. Your kids will love hearing the same jokes again and again—no matter how they moan and groan.

He will fill your mouth with laughter. Shouts of joy will come from your lips.

Job 8:21 NIrV

A cheerful heart is a good medicine.

Proverbs 17:22 NRSV

Give me a keen and ever present sense of humor; it is the next best thing to an abiding faith in providence.

George B. Cheever

In the Hollow of His Hand

Whoever listens to me will live in safety and be at ease, without fear of harm.

~ *Proverbs 1:33* NIV

Kevin and his family had returned to his parents' farm. His children loved to visit their grandparents and to explore the fields and woods their father had roamed as a child. On this visit, they discovered that the wild blueberries were ripe and ready for picking. The kids' baskets were full and their lips were stained blue by the time they had finished.

Suddenly, the skies filled with rolling black clouds and a deafening hailstorm swept across the south pasture toward them. "Run! This way!" Kevin shouted. With the kids on his heels, he dashed toward the creek, ran down a path, and ducked into a large cave in the side of the creek canyon. Seconds later, huge hailstones were hammering the ground outside the cave.

"Welcome to my secret fortress," Kevin said. He lit some dry wood and, as the storm raged outside, Kevin shared many happy memories of his childhood hiding place God had provided for him.

❧ As a young man fleeing his enemies, David took refuge in caves, and he later often referred to God as his hiding place and fortress. Three thousand years later, God is still the refuge you can flee to in prayer when you have troubles or need shelter from life's storms. God is able to protect you from danger and keep you from misfortune if you trust in him. Make him your refuge and teach your children how to go to him as well.

❧ TRY THIS: *Take your children with you to a store that sells posters and choose a picture of a mountain stronghold or castle on top of a rocky pinnacle. Hang it on the wall in your home to remind yourself and your children that God is your fortress. A Christian bookstore might even have a calendar like that with a Scripture on it.*

GOD HAS ALWAYS BEEN YOUR DEFENSE; HIS ETERNAL ARMS ARE YOUR SUPPORT.

DEUTERONOMY 33:27 GNT

HE SHALL COVER THEE WITH HIS FEATHERS, AND UNDER HIS WINGS SHALT THOU TRUST: HIS TRUTH SHALL BE THY SHIELD AND BUCKLER.

PSALM 91:4 KJV

It is only the fear of God that can deliver us from the fear of man.
JOHN WITHERSPOON

The Victorious Dad

Any boxer can boast when he wins a match,
And shout with his lip proudly curled,
But the man who has won, who has truly won,
Is the Christian who conquers the world.

Sure, it's hard to win a twelve-round bout,
But it's harder to live life right;
Victory worth having is the victory God gives
To the men who fight the good fight.

Ed Strauss

*The LORD holds victory
in store for the upright.*

— *Proverbs 2:7 NIV*

*Whosoever is born of
God overcometh the
world: and this is the
victory that overcometh
the world, even our faith.*

— *I John 5:4 KJV*

BLESSINGS EVER
WAIT ON VIRTUOUS
DEEDS, AND
THOUGH LATE, A
SURE REWARD
SUCCEEDS.

WILLIAM CONGREVE

SHOULDER TO SHOULDER

Kinsfolk are born to share adversity.

~ *Proverbs 17:17* NRSV

The McIntuck brothers had always been tight-knit. Ben knew that when he needed help or was in a tight situation, he could turn to his older brother, Stuart. So when Stuart lost his job, Ben was determined to help.

When Stuart's bills started stacking up, Ben loaned Stuart money to pay them. Lucy, Ben's wife, saw to it that Stuart's family had groceries. When Christmas came, Ben and his family sat down together to decide how they could help. Ben and Lucy's children suggested that they would share some of their own presents with their cousins.

The much-sought-after job came in early January. When he received his first check, Stuart's family invited Ben's family for a cookout to celebrate. Before eating, they bowed their heads and Ben prayed. "Lord, thank you for my brother and his wonderful family. Bless them for reaching out to us when we were in need. And help us be ready to help when they need us."

Sharing times of trouble with brothers and sisters in need can bring families closer together. Hard times also provide opportunity to demonstrate to your children what's important in life and what love looks like in action. If they see you giving cheerfully and generously, and helping without begrudging—and if they hear you expressing feelings of sincere love for your family, especially during hard times—those values of helping and generosity will be imprinted deeply in their lives.

Try this: *To help your children become inspired about giving to family members—or to needy families in your church—clearly explain the situation those people are in and the needs they have. Then walk through your house and ask your children for suggestions about items they can share with others.*

YOUR WORDS HELPED THOSE WHO HAD FALLEN DOWN. YOU MADE SHAKY KNEES STRONG.

JOB 4:4 NIRV

IF ONE FALLS DOWN, HIS FRIEND CAN HELP HIM UP . . . . THOUGH ONE MAY BE OVERPOWERED, TWO CAN DEFEND THEMSELVES.

ECCLESIASTES 4:10, 12 NIV

A friend should bear his friend's infirmities.

WILLIAM SHAKESPEARE

Those Who Went Before

A wise man listens to advice.

~ *Proverbs 12:15 NIV*

Grandpa Porter came by Scott and Margaret's house often, and he freely gave advice on how to fix the roof, rearrange the tool shed, and raise their children. Once while Henry was fixing the lawn mower, Grandpa spent two hours explaining to him how to vote in the upcoming municipal election. Sometimes Scott thought that Grandpa Porter's constant advice was annoying, but most of the time he knew it was on target.

After one visit, Scott's son, Martin, just shook his head in bewilderment. "Dad," he said, "you're thirty-five years old, and grandpa is still telling you what to do!"

Scott smiled. "Sometimes Grandpa is a bit outspoken, but he does have a lot of experience, doesn't he?"

Martin shrugged. "Yeah, but you're old enough to figure things out for yourself, aren't you?"

"Of course," Scott answered, "and I do. I've learned a lot from your grandfather, and I hope you're learning from my experience."

Good advice comes from many sources. One of the best places to learn life principles is your Bible. King Solomon wanted his son to be able to avoid the pitfalls he had stumbled into during his life, and he wanted him to have a reverential fear of God and to understand how to relate to God in a practical way. He wanted those things so badly that he took the time to write down his advice in the book of Proverbs.

Try this: Over dinner, tell your children a personal story of a specific time when following wise advice had a positive outcome. Point out the time, money, and effort you saved by heeding the advice. Keep the story upbeat and encourage your children to tell you what they think about it.

Get all the advice you can, and you will succeed; without it you will fail.

Proverbs 15:22 GNT

Listen to advice and accept instruction, and in the end you will be wise.

Proverbs 19:20 NIV

King David, who personally heard from God, listened to advisors older and wiser than himself. May we also have the humility to hear advice.

Kenneth P. Walters

49

TAKE A DEEP BREATH

He who is slow to anger is better than the mighty.

~ Proverbs 16:32 NASB

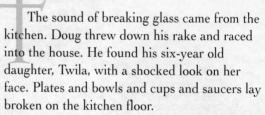

HE WHO CAN
SUPPRESS A
MOMENT'S ANGER
MAY PREVENT A
DAY OF SORROW.
TRYON EDWARDS

The sound of breaking glass came from the kitchen. Doug threw down his rake and raced into the house. He found his six-year old daughter, Twila, with a shocked look on her face. Plates and bowls and cups and saucers lay broken on the kitchen floor.

Doug was normally quick to anger. Not so long ago, his response might have been to shout, "Look what you've done!" Instead, he held his tongue, walked across the broken dishes, and carried his barefoot daughter to safety. "I was just trying to get a plate!" she wept.

"Let me get my breath," Doug whispered. He forced himself to think of his daughter's innocent motives; he reminded himself that he was truly thankful that she was not hurt. And the dishes could always be replaced. He set Twila down on the lawn outside. "Now, tell Daddy what happened," he said calmly and smiled.

❧ Anger in itself is not a sin because there are situations and injustices you should get angry about. Anger is a God-given emotion. Jesus himself was angry at times. But allowing the everyday frustrations and setbacks to leave you short-tempered and quick to anger is not productive. Rather than simply letting your emotions out unchecked, ask God to help you control them so that you can respond to problems in a way that will set a good example for your children.

❧ TRY THIS: *Whenever you're tempted to react in anger, count to twenty. If you're really upset, keep counting as you walk to the refrigerator. Take out an ice cube and calmly think about the incident without speaking until the ice cube melts in your hand. It will help you to cool down.*

A FOOL GIVES FULL VENT TO HIS ANGER, BUT A WISE MAN KEEPS HIMSELF UNDER CONTROL.

PROVERBS 29:11 NIV

EVERYONE SHOULD BE QUICK TO LISTEN, SLOW TO SPEAK, AND SLOW TO BECOME ANGRY, FOR MAN'S ANGER DOES NOT BRING ABOUT THE RIGHTEOUS LIFE THAT GOD DESIRES.

JAMES 1:19–20 NIV

When angry, count ten before you speak; if very angry, count a hundred.

THOMAS JEFFERSON

Taking Care of Business

Do you see a man skilled in his work? He will serve before kings.

~ *Proverbs 22:29* NIV

ONE TODAY IS
WORTH TWO
TOMORROWS;
NEVER LEAVE
THAT TILL
TOMORROW
WHICH YOU CAN
DO TODAY.

BENJAMIN FRANKLIN

James was a natural-born people person, and he needed that skill as a salesman for Superior Auto Parts. He was diligent, hard working, and dedicated to doing the best job he could do. One day an oil-splattered man came in wanting an obscure engine part for an antique car he was restoring. James checked his computer and told the man, "Sorry, they don't make those any more." He added, "But leave me your name and phone number. Some company somewhere might still have it in stock."

When he had some free time, James checked several old catalogs, made phone calls to follow up on leads, and was pleased to finally find the part. He knew how good he would feel when he called the man with the news of his success.

When James called with the news, however, the man seemed only vaguely pleased. Still, James knew he had done the right thing in going the extra mile for his customer.

🌿 Hard work and diligence are two of the attributes most needed for success, especially in business. You will be doing your children a great service if you help them develop disciplined work habits and take pride in a job well done at a young age. Most kids learn best when words and actions come together. So count on your example to play a big role in teaching your children the benefits of hard work.

🌿 TRY THIS: *Choose a task that you and your children can tackle together—cleaning the garage, washing the car, or cleaning the windows. Provide plenty of hands-on instruction and a solid example. When the job is finished, celebrate with a reward proportionate to the task—a trip to the store for some ice cream, for example.*

BEING LAZY WILL MAKE YOU POOR, BUT HARD WORK WILL MAKE YOU RICH.

PROVERBS 10:4 GNT

ALL HARD WORK PAYS OFF. BUT IF ALL YOU DO IS TALK, YOU WILL BE POOR.

PROVERBS 14:23 NIRV

Genius begins great works; labor alone finishes them.

JOSEPH JOUBERT

The Loving Dad

Sure, dad corrected my childish sins
And reproved me when I was wrong,
But he always dealt with me in love
'Cause his love was deep and strong.

He showed his love in a thousand ways,
It was proved to me over and again;
He was not rich, but his heart was great,
And he stood as a prince among men.

Ed Strauss

*Love covers over
all wrongs.*

~ *Proverbs 10:12 NIV*

*The LORD gathers the
lambs in his arms. He
carries them close
to his heart.*

~ *Isaiah 40:11 NIrV*

IF THERE IS
ANYTHING BETTER
THAN TO BE LOVED
IT IS LOVING.

AUTHOR UNKNOWN

Pointing the Way

Train a child in the way he should go, and when he is old he will not turn from it.

~ *Proverbs 22:6 NIV*

While Mom stayed at the cabin, Harold and his children went on a wilderness hike through a large state park. Today they had explored a beautiful creek and followed it some way downstream before heading back to the path. That's when they realized that they were lost.

At first the two younger children, Molly and Timmy, were frightened. But Tony and Marie had learned from their father, and Harold watched with pride as they took over. After reassuring his two younger siblings, Tony sat down on the grass with the compass and map and pinpointed their location, then jumped up to lead the way out of the park.

"I'll look for landmarks!" Marie said. "I saw a big pine tree near the trail." And sure enough, within a few minutes Marie had spotted the tree and about twenty yards below them, the path. Harold patted his daughter's shoulder and beamed at his son—they had learned the lessons of leadership.

꙳ Your children are looking to you as a spiritual leader. It's necessary and good to teach them what God's Word says, to define godly values and behavioral guidelines, and to take decisive action based on those truths. You need to enforce rules of godly behavior and, when it comes to gray areas, decide what is right and wrong. That's what leadership is all about. If you set an example of strong spiritual leadership, your children will learn to lead others as well.

꙳ TRY THIS: *To give your children opportunities to practice leadership—and to understand how you make decisions that affect them—write down different scenarios, then let each child take a turn being "leader" and making decisions. For example, you might have one of your children make assignments in preparation for a family vacation.*

BE AN EXAMPLE FOR THE BELIEVERS IN YOUR SPEECH, YOUR CONDUCT, YOUR LOVE, FAITH, AND PURITY.

1 TIMOTHY 4:12 GNT

BE YE FOLLOWERS OF ME, AS I ALSO AM OF CHRIST.

1 CORINTHIANS 11:1 KJV

The hand of the parent writes on the heart of the child the first faint characters which time deepens into strength so that nothing can efface them.

ROWLAND HILL

Take a Break

Better a little with the fear of the LORD than great wealth with turmoil.

~ *Proverbs* 15:16 NIV

God never built a Christian strong enough to carry today's duties and tomorrow's anxieties piled on the top of them.

Theodore L. Cuyler

Andy was a professional house painter, and he was usually quite able to make ends meet with the jobs he landed. During one particularly slow period, however, he had to take a second job cleaning offices at night. Not long after he started moonlighting, however, he landed a huge painting project with a very short deadline. Stress was building, and Andy was feeling it.

One evening as Andy was heating up some food in the microwave oven, he noticed a message by the phone. "Your brother would like for you to go fishing with him on Saturday." Andy frowned. Saturday? A coworker had offered him an additional cleaning job that day.

Andy sat down at the kitchen table and stared at his steaming food. He wanted the extra money, but he also knew that he needed a break. He needed to relax and trust God was in charge of his finances and his family. Then he made his decision. He went fishing.

꙾ Taking on extra work is practically guaranteed to add stress to your life. At times this can't be helped—you may need to take a second job just to pay your bills. However, you should learn when to call it quits. Your body, mind, and spirit need times of relaxation to recharge. Use the time to be with family, participate in relaxing activities, and invest in your relationship with God. Focus on things that will decrease your stress level.

꙾ TRY THIS: *In the same way that you might create a budget for your money, sit down with pencil and paper to create a budget for your time. Along with eating, sleeping, and working, be sure to include time for God, for your family, and for yourself. Avoid skimping on yourself in order to "save" time.*

DO NOT WEARY YOURSELF TO GAIN WEALTH, CEASE FROM YOUR CONSIDERATION OF IT.

PROVERBS 23:4 NASB

CAST ALL YOUR ANXIETY ON GOD BECAUSE HE CARES FOR YOU.

I PETER 5:7 NIV

Money never made a man happy yet, nor will it. If it satisfies one want, it doubles and trebles that want another way.

BENJAMIN FRANKLIN

It's How You Say It

Pleasant words are like a honeycomb, sweetness to the soul and health to the body.

~ *Proverbs 16:24 NRSV*

Steve sat in the darkened auditorium watching his fourteen-year-old daughter, Marisha, perform at dress rehearsal. He was pleased that she had a starring role in her school play and had worked so hard to do her very best.

On the way home Steve was surprised when Marisha broke into tears. "I just can't get my lines right," she sobbed. "I keep stumbling over the same few words. What if I mess up again tomorrow night?"

Steve reached over and squeezed his daughter's arm. "I was there tonight, remember? You may have missed a few words, but I couldn't tell. Your acting was powerful and full of emotion. I thought you were terrific. You did just fine tonight and you'll do it again tomorrow night! Dads know these things."

The next night, Marisha delivered a great performance. As the curtains closed and the audience clapped and shouted "Bravo!" she caught her dad's eye in the audience and gave him a huge smile.

60

You are probably your kids' biggest fan in all their activities, and as they face discouragements and obstacles, your words of encouragement will help to keep them from giving up. Make sure your words are genuine; your kids will know if you're faking it—even if they know you're doing it out of love. In the face of a significant disaster, however, there is almost always some positive aspect you can point to. You'll see it if you're looking.

TRY THIS: *One Saturday morning a month, take one of your children out to breakfast. Let your child choose the place. Use the time together to listen to your child's life updates and take every single opportunity that presents itself to encourage your child through difficulties and disappointments and applaud him or her for victories and accomplishments.*

JOSEPH REASSURED THEM WITH KIND WORDS THAT TOUCHED THEIR HEARTS.

GENESIS 50:21 GNT

THE SOVEREIGN LORD HAS GIVEN ME AN INSTRUCTED TONGUE, TO KNOW THE WORD THAT SUSTAINS THE WEARY.

ISAIAH 50:4 NIV

Words are not "mere nothings." Time and again, encouraging words spoken to a weary person have spurred them on to complete some world-changing deed.

CHARLES W. FOXE

61

The Last Shall Be First

Pride goeth before destruction, and an haughty spirit before a fall.

~ *Proverbs 16:18* KJV

He that is proud eats up himself.

William Shakespeare

Bill's party supply store had just about every kind of balloon, party goods, banners, and clown supply you could imagine—plus Bill's three older children acted as part-time clowns and decorated houses for parties. There was simply nothing to compare with their products and service. Bill soon boasted that people from five counties came to him for party supplies and clowns.

That's why Bill didn't feel he needed to listen to Jeanette, his oldest child and most talented clown and decorator. Jeanette had many great ideas and suggestions, but Bill didn't feel the need to revamp a highly successful business because of a few suggestions from a high-school student. Jeanette soon became frustrated and lost interest.

Noting the change in Jeanette, Bill finally realized he had to rethink his way of planning future expansion. Bill had been guilty of devaluing the contributions that Jeanette and his other children were making to the business. He resolved to set aside regular time for all of them to discuss their ideas.

A sense of achievement is great, but if you let your accomplishments go to your head, you could be setting yourself up for a fall. Pride can make you defensive and closed to change. Make sure pride doesn't write the last chapter of your success story. Nip it in the bud. Stop it in its tracks. Avoid it at all costs. Pride doesn't pay, but a humble assessment of yourself does. Let humility help you preserve what you have worked so hard to gain.

TRY THIS: *Examine a few of your past accomplishments and list all the people who contributed to your success — your wife, for instance, who made sure you could work undisturbed; your secretary, who worked overtime to finish your reports; your junior colleague, whose chance comment sent you in the right direction. Now think of how far you could have gone without their help.*

BEFORE HONOR COMES HUMILITY.

PROVERBS 15:33
NASB

IF A MAN IS PROUD, HE WILL BE MADE LOW. BUT IF HE ISN'T PROUD, HE WILL BE HONORED.

PROVERBS 29:23
NIRV

Pride defeats its own end, by bringing the man who seeks esteem and reverence into contempt.

LORD HENRY BOLINGBROKE

The Merciful Dad

It wasn't a fact that newspapers blazed,

No, it wasn't that big of a thing—

When my father gave me another chance,

When he mended a bluebird's wing,

When he gave to the poor and homeless,

And forgave the mistakes of a friend—

Yet lessons of mercy were

printed on my heart

By my father again and again.

ED STRAUSS

The merciful man doeth good to his own soul.

~ *Proverbs 11:17* KJV

Jesus said, "Blessed are the merciful, for they shall receive mercy."

~ *Matthew 5:7* NASB

WE DO PRAY FOR MERCY, AND THAT SAME PRAYER DOTH TEACH US ALL TO RENDER THE DEEDS OF MERCY.

WILLIAM SHAKESPEARE

I'm Proud of You, Dad

The man of integrity walks securely.

~ *Proverbs 10:9 NIV*

Two of Greg's workmates liked to boast how they "saved" hundreds of dollars by bootlegging copyrighted computer programs. They repeatedly offered to load copies on Greg's home computer and couldn't understand how he could refuse. One even mentioned it in front of Greg's kids. "But Dad, why won't you let him do it?" they asked. Greg quietly explained that such an action might jeopardize his job, and it would definitely jeopardize his integrity.

Then one day their company's computer technician called everyone into his office and warned them about bootlegging software. Every worker, Greg included, looked him in the eye and could assure him they had never done that nor would they.

Two weeks later Greg's home computer malfunctioned and the company's computer technician offered to get it up and running for him as a favor. Greg's kids were grinning from ear to ear when he explained to them that he was able to accept the offer because he had nothing to hide.

It may not seem like they are, but your children are watching you. They are watching the way you handle conflict and disappointment. They are noticing your attitudes, behaviors, and reactions to the world around you. Make sure your children see integrity in your life. What they see you doing, the things that make them proud of you, may be the very things that will make you proud of them one day. Do the right thing for their sakes as well as your own.

TRY THIS: *Give each of your school-age children a piece of paper with a line drawn down the middle. Ask each one to write on the left side any wrong things they are tempted to do, and on the right side any consequences if they give in. Discuss.*

MAY INTEGRITY AND UPRIGHTNESS PRESERVE ME, FOR I WAIT FOR YOU.

PSALMS 25:21 NRSV

THE JUST MAN WALKETH IN HIS INTEGRITY: HIS CHILDREN ARE BLESSED AFTER HIM.

PROVERBS 20:7 KJV

In all things preserve integrity; and the consciousness of thine own uprightness will . . . give thee a humble confidence before God.

WILLIAM PALEY

Tune In

The wise of heart is called perceptive.

~ *Proverbs 16:21 NRSV*

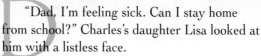

Insight is seeing with the sight and the mind.

Kenneth P. Walters

"Dad, I'm feeling sick. Can I stay home from school?" Charles's daughter Lisa looked at him with a listless face.

"Sick?" he asked. "Describe sick," Charles probed.

"I don't know for sure. I think I just need to stay home and rest," Lisa explained.

Charles felt her forehead. He could see that something about this wasn't quite right. "Is everything okay in school?" he asked. Lisa looked down and mumbled, "Sure."

Charles pursued the line of questioning, and eventually she confessed that a girl in her class was bullying her and making her life miserable. She dreaded another day of being intimidated by that girl. A tear escaped her eye.

Charles hugged his daughter. "Come on honey," he said. "You don't have to figure this out by yourself. We'll ask God what to do, and then we'll settle on a plan."

"Thanks, Dad," Lisa said, smiling through her tears. "You always know how to make me feel better."

When children are young they're open about their feelings, but as they grow older they're not always so forthright. Perhaps pride, embarrassment, guilt, or shyness keeps them from telling you the whole story. If you want to help them, it's important to try to understand not only what they're saying, but what they're not saying. Pray often for the kind of insight that will make it possible for you to help your children through their difficult times.

Try this: Come up with three questions to ask yourself the next time your child leaves you baffled and wondering: (1) What does he mean by that? (2) Is something happening in her life that I should know about? (3) Am I making myself as approachable as possible?

GIVE YOUR SERVANT A DISCERNING HEART TO GOVERN YOUR PEOPLE AND TO DISTINGUISH BETWEEN RIGHT AND WRONG.

I KINGS 3:9 NIV

A WISE MAN'S HEART DISCERNETH BOTH TIME AND JUDGMENT.

ECCLESIASTES 8:5 KJV

Discernment is a practiced grace. Hebrews 5:14 praises those "who by reason of use have their senses exercised to discern both good and evil."

CHARLES W. FOXE

Making a Mark

A good man leaves an inheritance to his children's children.

~ *Proverbs* 13:22 NASB

NO LEGACY IS SO
RICH AS HONESTY.
William
Shakespeare

Philip and his two children, Joey and Annie, were snuggled on the living room couch watching a television documentary called "The Legacy of Lincoln." At the end of the program, the camera showed people filing slowly and respectfully past the Lincoln Memorial in Washington, D.C.

Philip served his children a bedtime snack as snow fell softly outside the house. Joey paused while munching on a cookie and asked, "Dad, what's your legacy going to be?"

Philip smiled. "I hope people will remember me as a man who loved God, a man who was a good father, a faithful husband, and a hard worker, and a man who helped others as much as he could."

The next day when Philip came home from work his children led him to the backyard. "Surprise!" Annie announced. Seated on a snow chair was a larger-than-life snow dad with Philip's legacy scrawled on a makeshift sign in felt markers.

Everyone will leave a legacy, because you will be remembered for how you lived. You may not feel that you've accomplished anything particularly outstanding in your life, but your legacy is the sum total of who you are, the values you stand for, and the accomplishments you have managed. Your influence, unaffected by wealth or possessions or fame, will live on in the lives of your children and grandchildren.

Try this: *Take a small piece of paper and paper-clip it to your will. At the top, write* THREE THINGS I WISH MY CHILDREN TO SAY ABOUT ME AFTER I PASS AWAY. *Write down three statements beginning with "My dad was —" and then strive to live your life so they will have reason to say those things.*

GOOD PEOPLE WILL BE REMEMBERED AS A BLESSING.

PROVERBS 10:7 GNT

A RIGHTEOUS MAN WHO WALKS IN HIS INTEGRITY—HOW BLESSED ARE HIS SONS AFTER HIM.

PROVERBS 20:7 NASB

Think of what impressed you about your parents. Think of the impression you are making upon your own children. That is legacy.

AUTHOR UNKNOWN

Next Time

*People who promise things that they never give are like clouds
and wind that bring no rain.*

~ *Proverbs 25:14 GNT*

A MIND
CONSCIOUS OF
INTEGRITY
SCORNS TO SAY
MORE THAN IT
MEANS TO
PERFORM.

ROBERT BURNS

Gordon was awakened early one Saturday
morning by his sons excitedly clambering on top
of him and shaking him. "It's time to get up,
Daddy!" said Harry. "We've got to get ready!
We've got to go to Bumper Cars Stadium!" His
brother, Chris, began tugging on the covers and
pulling them off his father.

Gordon drowsily opened his eyes. "Boys,
boys. Daddy's trying to sleep. We stayed up late
last night watching a video, remember? I need
to sleep some more.

Chris said, "But you promised last week we
could go to Bumper Cars Stadium Saturday
morning."

"Oh, yeah . . . I did," Gordon mumbled.
He was about to say, "Listen boys, can we go
next Saturday?" when he suddenly remembered
what that had felt like when his father said the
same thing. Gordon sat up in bed and swung his
legs to the side with an effort of sheer will
power. He wasn't going to break a promise to
his sons once again.

If you make a promise to your children, do your best to follow through on it. When you keep your promise you're sending the message to your children that sticking by your word is important. Pause and think carefully before you make a promise. Make sure your time is not already booked. If you're not sure if something can happen, qualify your commitment: "We'll do this unless—." That way, you will be far more likely to be able to keep your promise.

❧ *Try this: If you don't have a calendar in your kitchen, put one up. Then buy some bright, fluorescent sticky notes. Whenever you make a promise to your children, write it on the note and stick it on the calendar. This will be a visible reminder to both you and your children about the promise made.*

Finish the arrangements for the generous gift you had promised. Then it will be ready as a generous gift.

2 Corinthians 9:5
NIV

It is better to make no promise at all than to make a promise and not keep it.

Ecclesiastes 5:5
NIrV

In religion not to do as thou sayest is to unsay thy religion in thy deeds, and to undo thyself.

Ralph Venning

73

The Patient Dad

Ah! Patience is a wonderful virtue

That makes a poor man a king;

You can rise above men of furious strength

If you can but wait for a thing.

If you're patient you won't curse the storm

When you sail on a sea of strife;

You'll calmly endure lesser men's jeers,

When patience gives strength to your life.

Ed Strauss

*A patient man calms
a quarrel.*

~ *Proverbs 15:18 NIV*

*Encourage the
fainthearted, help the weak,
be patient with all of them.*

~ *1 Thessalonians 5:14 NRSV*

Be patient in
little things.
Learn to bear
the everyday
trials and
annoyances of
life quietly and
calmly, and
then, when
unforeseen
trouble or
calamity comes,
your strength
will not
forsake you.

William S. Plumer

Start a Habit

Every word of God proves true; he is a shield to those who take refuge in him.

~ *Proverbs* 30:5 NRSV

The sun had set over Elk Canyon State Park and the campfire had burned down. Keith put the food away in the cooler while the boys brushed their teeth. Keith was exhausted—it had been a long and busy day—but he pumped up the kerosene lamp, set it on the picnic table, and pulled out his Bible.

As a moth danced around the bright light, Keith started to read. Only a week ago he had made a resolution to read his Bible from beginning to end, but he had wanted to skip it during this camping trip. Even so, he knew he needed to be faithful.

As Keith began reading the story of how Jacob got Isaac's blessing, Keith's younger son stepped through the tent flap and saw him sitting there. "Hey, Dad, you're keeping your resolution," he said, grinning. "And it's not even New Year's."

It takes time to establish a Bible-reading habit—just like establishing an exercise routine. First, weigh the pros and the cons to convince yourself that you need to read the Bible faithfully. Second, figure out what's stopping you and determine to overcome it. Third, come up with a plan of exactly how and when you'll do it, promise yourself you will do it, and tell others about your commitment. Then, fourth, go for it and stick to it.

Try this: *At the top of a sheet of paper write READING MY BIBLE FAITHFULLY. Make a chart to track the date, pages read or hours spent, with space for comments or key Scripture verses that have special meaning to you. As times goes by, take time to reflect on your progress and the insight you have gained since you began.*

Day after day, from the first day to the last, Ezra read from the book of the Law of God.

Nehemiah 8:18 niv

Give attendance to reading, to exhortation, to doctrine. . . . Meditate upon these things; give thyself wholly to them; that thy profiting may appear to all.

I Timothy 4:13, 15 KJV

I have read the Bible through many times, and now make it a practice to read it though once every year.

Daniel Webster

A Sleepless Night

When you lie down, you won't be afraid.

~ *Proverbs 3:24 NIrV*

Bert's mind was restless. He needed sleep, but he couldn't quiet the turmoil in his emotions. The doctors had diagnosed his son Kenny as having diabetes two days ago, and Kenny had started taking insulin injections. It seemed to be such an abrupt change, and Kenny's condition initiated a steep learning curve for the whole family. From now on, they'd have to watch his diet, watch his blood sugar level, and a hundred other things. It was a lot to take in. And now, although he had lain awake praying for an hour, he couldn't stop his mind from racing.

Bert turned over in bed. Thankfully they had discovered Kenny's condition and they were doing everything they could to manage it. *I need to get some sleep*, he thought. *I'm just going to have to trust God*. He committed his son's health to the Lord, put the whole matter in the Lord's hands, and finally fell asleep.

The Bible tells you to "cast all your anxiety on him," then adds a good reason to do that: "because he cares for you" (1 Peter 5:7). That's why you can stop lying awake all night and start getting some sleep. Notice the word *cast*. If you have trouble with insomnia—and there's not some physical cause, it's just concern and anxiety—then you need to make a conscious choice to pick those cares off your shoulders and heave them onto God's shoulders.

Try this: If you lie awake in bed for hours praying and thinking, make a decision to get out of bed to pray. List all the things that worry you and then kneel beside your bed, commit everything to God, and check them off on your list. Tell yourself, "I've finished praying. Now I'm going to bed to sleep."

When I lie down, I go to sleep in peace; you alone, O Lord, keep me perfectly safe.

Psalm 4:8 GNT

The Lord grants sleep to those he loves.

Psalm 127:2 NIV

Sleep dwell upon thine eyes, peace in thy breast!

William Shakespeare

Listen Up

Like a gold ring or an ornament of gold is a wise rebuke to a listening ear.

~ *Proverbs* 25:12 NRSV

HE THAT WON'T
BE COUNSELED
CAN'T BE HELPED.
Benjamin Franklin

Bob was a forklift driver in a lumber mill. He had nine years of experience and was proud of his abilities. But when he moved his family to Washington State, Bob had to look for a new job. Not only did he lose his seniority, but his new boss often had a different way of doing things than Bob was used to. It was humbling—and sometimes even humiliating—to be told constantly how to do tasks that he was adept at performing.

A week into his new job, Bob arrived at work to find the boss in a serious mood. "You didn't follow my instructions," he sighed. He marched Bob out into the lumberyard and explained that the pallets were too high and that he'd have to restack them. "You simply must follow safety regulations," he emphasized.

Bob was tempted to argue, but he didn't. Instead, he said, "You're right. They are too high. I'll get on it right now."

80

When you see your children do dangerous things, adults often find it easy to tell them to stop. And sometimes adults use a not-too-gracious tone of voice. You know that safety is a serious matter and that you're right to expect them to listen and obey. That same principle should hold true in your own life. If you're receiving wise advice or instructions at your workplace or any other place, learn to value it, even if it's given in a blunt manner.

TRY THIS: *If you're receiving correction and reproofs in your workplace, put a bandage on a finger to remind you that you that you must listen and do things a certain way, whether for safety or for company efficiency. If you work at a computer and a bandaged finger would be awkward, attach your reminder to the side of your monitor.*

REPROOFS FOR DISCIPLINE ARE THE WAY OF LIFE.

PROVERBS 6:23 NASB

WHOEVER HEEDS INSTRUCTION IS ON THE PATH TO LIFE, BUT ONE WHO REJECTS A REBUKE GOES ASTRAY.

PROVERBS 10:17 NRSV

A proud man won't listen to correction; it is only the humble man who listens and acts on correction who improves himself.

CHARLES W. FOXE

Eating Right

The righteous [man] has enough to satisfy his appetite.

~ *Proverbs 13:25 NASB*

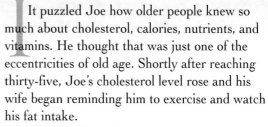

It puzzled Joe how older people knew so much about cholesterol, calories, nutrients, and vitamins. He thought that was just one of the eccentricities of old age. Shortly after reaching thirty-five, Joe's cholesterol level rose and his wife began reminding him to exercise and watch his fat intake.

He might have been tempted to ignore her if he hadn't looked in the mirror one day and realized that he had a paunch. Joe had never watched his eating habits, but he realized that he needed to change. He started by reading up on cholesterol and found out what kind of foods he needed to avoid.

Within a few months he had almost entirely quit fast foods and had discovered the world of salad bars. Even his kids learned to appreciate the tasty new foods that he and his wife added to the family menu. He was glad to see them adapting easily to their healthier lifestyle.

There's a lot of truth to the fact that a simple Mediterranean diet—the kind Jesus and his disciples ate—is good for your heath. You may be at a point in your life where you often have to eat and run, but you can still eat more healthily and regulate your intake. Choosing to eat foods that are good for you means that you'll live longer, be sick less often, and have more energy.

TRY THIS: *To remind yourself to eat healthy food, get the whole family involved—including whoever does the grocery shopping in your house. Teach your children to read the nutrition information labels so they can learn early in life what healthy cholesterol, fat and calorie levels are . . . and be sure you stock up on healthy foods for those in-between meal snacks at work and home.*

IF YOU FIND HONEY, EAT JUST ENOUGH.

PROVERBS 25:16 NIV

I PRAY YOU TO TAKE SOME MEAT: FOR THIS IS FOR YOUR HEALTH.

ACTS 27:34 KJV

An apple a day keeps the doctor away.

AMERICAN PROVERB

The Wise Dad

He didn't have a college education, my dad,

And he couldn't quote Latin or Greek,

But he knew what mattered the most in life;

He was deep and knew when to speak.

When we kids grew up we stayed in touch

And we often called home for advice,

'Cause our dad could see

to the heart of things

In ways that were simple but wise.

Ed Strauss

A wise man has great power, and a man of knowledge increases strength.

— *Proverbs 24:5 NIV*

If any of you lack wisdom, you should pray to God, who will give it to you; because God gives generously and graciously to all.

— *James 1:5 GNT*

TO KNOW HOW TO
USE KNOWLEDGE IS
TO HAVE WISDOM.

CHARLES SPURGEON

THE POWER OF WORDS

The tongue of the righteous is choice silver

~ *Proverbs* 10:20 NRSV

It is not only what you say but how you say it that counts.

AMERICAN PROVERB

Matt Atkins had just taken out the trash when a car full of teens swerved sharply up the driveway, hitting both trash cans and scattering their contents in the street. The car stopped short of the garage, and Matt's son, Chip, jumped out of the driver's side. Four kids from Chip's youth group silently piled out of the car.

"I think we need to have a talk, son," Matt said in a calm voice. He turned to the other teens. "Why don't you go on inside? Matt and I need to clean up this mess."

Chip was extremely relieved that his dad hadn't rebuked him in front of the other teens. Even when they sat down to talk privately and seriously, Matt didn't tear into him. Chip was impressed not only by what his dad said but also by the tone in which he said it. Chip apologized and immediately promised to never do anything so reckless again.

It's easy to be gracious and understanding when others are discouraged and need cheering on, or when they're grieving and need to be consoled. It's easy to reassure your children when they are fearful. Unpleasant times—when your child has either disappointed or disobeyed you—give you some of the best opportunities to speak loving, encouraging words. When these opportunities happen, you must pray for wisdom, weigh your words most carefully, and consider the long-term effect of your words on your children.

TRY THIS: *Write the sentence "Speak encouraging words" in hollow letters, or print them out on your computer. If your children are young enough, get them to color it. Then put the saying up in a conspicuous space in your house. This will not only remind you to watch what you say but will be good for your kids as well.*

THE TONGUE OF THE WISE BRINGS HEALING.

PROVERBS 12:18 NASB

THE TONGUE HAS THE POWER OF LIFE AND DEATH, AND THOSE WHO LOVE IT WILL EAT ITS FRUIT.

PROVERBS 18:21 NIV

If men would only think through what they said, and the effect it would have on those they're speaking to, many problems would be solved before they started.

KENNETH P. WALTERS

Just Being Together

The righteous give and do not hold back.

— *Proverbs 21:26* NRSV

WHAT A MAN
DOES WITH HIS
TIME AND HIS
MONEY IS THE
TRUEST
THERMOMETER
OF HIS HEART.

CHARLES W. FOXE

Chuck was tired from a long day at work and looked forward to watching some TV. As his wife walked outside to work in the garden, she assured him that their four-year old daughter, Melissa, would play quietly by herself. But no sooner had Chuck hit the couch than she asked him to help her build a castle out of LEGO bricks.

The thought of playing with LEGO bricks didn't appeal to Chuck, but he knew how much Melissa loved them. So he rolled off the couch to the floor and asked, "What'll we build today, sweetheart?" His daughter was delighted.

Later, Melissa grabbed her favorite book, climbed up on her dad's lap and asked him to read it. Chuck still hadn't caught a half-hour of TV yet, but he realized that he didn't want to miss this opportunity to spend quality time with his daughter. The joy on his daughter's face was his reward.

After a day's work you often feel a need to unwind; sometimes playing a game with your kids or doing an activity with them can resemble work more so than relaxation. This is especially true if you had planned on doing something else. You do need time for yourself, but spending time with your children is one of the surest ways to bond deeply with them and to communicate to them that you love them.

Try this: Keep a written record of how many minutes you spend with your children each day — how much time you spend with each child individually and how much time with them all together. If you find the results low, make a commitment to increase the time.

If you wish your children to give God their attention and love, give the same to them.

KENNETH P. WALTERS

LEADING YOUR CHILD TO CHRIST

The fruit of the righteous is a tree of life; and he that winneth souls is wise.

~ *Proverbs 11:30 KJV*

ONE TRULY CHRISTIAN LIFE WILL DO MORE TO PROVE THE DIVINE ORIGIN OF CHRISTIANITY THAN MANY LECTURES.

JOHN M. GIBSON

Ben and Gail had read their son Bible stories ever since he was a toddler. By the time he was five, Davie was familiar with the Bible. Recently Ben had been helping him understand why Jesus had to die on the cross to pay the price for sin.

Today they were spending the day on the beach, walking among the driftwood and shells, splashing along the shoreline, and feeling the sand and pebbles under their bare feet. Happily tired as dusk began to settle, they sat around a campfire, watching the glowing embers. Davie sat on a log between Ben and Gail. He looked up at the sky full of stars. Ben had been watching and listening to Davie all day, and he knew the time was right.

"Would you like to ask Jesus to come into your heart and to forgive your sins?" Ben asked.

David pursed his lips and nodded his head. "Yes," he said.

Leading your children to accept Jesus as their Savior is more than just sitting down with them and having them repeat a sinner's prayer. For the prayer to be meaningful and for it to change their lives, your children need to clearly understand why they are doing it. This involves grounding them in the Bible's truths, teaching them to pray, and modeling Christian virtues in your own life. Once they pray and give their lives to Jesus, the seed will take root in their lives.

Try this: *Mark the spiritual birthdays of all family members on a calendar, talk about the significance of these days as they approach, and then celebrate them with cake and candles. Celebrating each person's decision will give you opportunities to discuss and reinforce your children's commitment.*

Jesus said, "Let the little children come to me, and do not hinder them, for the kingdom of heaven belongs to such as these."

Matthew 19:14 NIV

You have known the Holy Scriptures ever since you were a little child. They are able to teach you how to be saved by believing in Christ Jesus.

2 Timothy 3:15 NIrV

Conversion is a deep work — a heart-work. It goes throughout the man, through the mind, through the members, throughout the entire life.

Joseph Alleine

Lending a Hand

One who is gracious to a poor man lends to the LORD.

~ *Proverbs 19:17* NASB

A MAN THERE WAS, AND THEY CALLED HIM MAD; THE MORE HE GAVE, THE MORE HE HAD.

JOHN BUNYAN

Dumitru and Adriana Ciocaltea and their children recently emigrated from Romania. Don and his wife, Sylvia, met them at church and befriended them. They soon found out that the Ciocalteas were having difficulty finding jobs and were struggling to make ends meet.

As they drove home from church one day, Don earnestly told Sylvia that he felt that God wanted them to help the new family. "We don't have a lot to spare," he admitted, "but I feel we could give them fifty dollars. What do you think, hon?" Sylvia smiled at Don and readily agreed.

"Dumitru needs a job," Don continued excitedly. "I could help him type a résumé and give him hints on interviewing."

"And I could take Adriana grocery shopping with me, help her find her way around the store," Sylvia said.

Don and Sylvia's oldest daughter, Brianna, suddenly piped up. "That's great, dad! And their daughter is my size. I could give her some of my clothes!"

🌿 Counsel with your kids and let them know that if you are able to physically help someone, you will, but if you can't, that you will at least pray for their needs, or put them in contact with people who can help them. When you know that God wants you to help someone and you do, you get a great feeling. Giving is contagious: when your children see you happy to give and happy to help others, they develop the same attitude.

🌿 TRY THIS: *Keep a Pray & Help three-ring binder where you can write down people's names and needs, and what your family has done to help them. Buy a box of sticky dots and color-code your family's efforts, such as a green dot for "gave money," a red dot for "prayed for their needs," and a blue dot for "other help."*

[A GOOD PERSON] GIVES GENEROUSLY TO THE NEEDY, AND HIS KINDNESS NEVER FAILS; HE WILL BE POWERFUL AND RESPECTED.

PSALM 112:9 GNT

EVEN THOUGH THEY WERE VERY POOR, THEY GAVE VERY FREELY.

2 CORINTHIANS 8:2 NIRV

It is not enough to help the feeble up, but to support him after.

WILLIAM SHAKESPEARE

The Enthusiastic Dad

Dad leaped to his feet in the baseball stands
When my bat slammed the ball up to Mars;
He whooped when I reeled in
a five-pound bass,
He cheered when I cleaned both the cars.
Whatever my dad did he did with a zest,
He lived eighty minutes each hour;
His enthusiastic ways day after day
Gave his life a great measure of power.

Ed Strauss

A joyful heart is good medicine.

— *Proverbs 17:22* NASB

It is fine to be zealous, provided the purpose is good.

— *Galations 4:18* NIV

GREAT DESIGNS ARE NOT ACCOMPLISHED WITHOUT ENTHUSIASM OF SOME SORT. IT IS THE INSPIRATION OF EVERYTHING GREAT.

CHRISTIAN BOVEE

Hugs and Kisses

Better is open rebuke than hidden love.

~ *Proverbs* 27:5 NIV

When we first bend over the cradle of our own child, God . . . reveals to us the sacredness and mystery of a father's and a mother's love to ourselves.

Henry Ward Beecher

Alex Walker stepped in the door of his house, draped his coat over the banister, threw out his arms, and bellowed, "Ho, ho, ho! Big old Shaggy Bear is home! Where are the Munchkins?" As Alex's coworker watched, twin six-year-old boys whooped excitedly and jumped up in Alex's arms.

Alex's nine-year-old daughter, Suzanne, quickly descended the stairs. "Dad!" She threw her arms around her father's neck and kissed his cheek.

A moment later, Alex's wife appeared and kissed him warmly. "We've missed you," she said.

Alex's coworker was impressed with the open and uninhibited show of affection. "And you were only gone for a weekend," he said. "Good thing we didn't stay away any longer!"

Before bedtime, Alex and his wife cuddled on the couch while their kids snuggled around them, and listened to his stories. Later Alex carried the twins upstairs, with Suzanne riding piggyback. Then he tucked them all into bed with a hug, a kiss, and a prayer.

Some people are more inclined to open, public displays of emotion than others, and while you may be more quiet and calm, it's nevertheless important to show affection to your children. Hugs and kisses should be part of their daily diet. They are visible, tangible proof to your children that you think they have value and that you love them. Frequent hugs and kisses also show that even though you must discipline your children from time to time, you still love them. Children need that reminder.

Try this: Promise yourself today that you will show your children more affection, and then make a point of hugging them when you sit on the couch together. If they're young, hug and kiss them every night before bed. If they're older, try pats on the shoulder.

Early in the morning Laban rose up, and kissed his grandchildren and his daughters and blessed them.

Genesis 31:55 NRSV

Greet one another with a kiss of love.

1 Peter 5:14 NIV

Kisses are like grains of gold or silver found upon the ground, of no value themselves, but precious as showing that a mine is near.

George Villiers

Everything in Its Place

Some people pretend to be rich but have nothing. Others pretend to be poor but have great wealth.

~ *Proverbs 13:7 NIRV*

Bruce and Loretta struggled financially for years. They both worked outside the home, and it often felt like they were dog-paddling to stay afloat financially. They bought their furniture and clothes in thrift stores, and Loretta, armed with grocery coupons, learned to become an expert shopper and a frugal meal planner. Despite their financial challenges, they gave to their church what they could and helped support a missionary.

By the time their kids were in their early teens, Bruce's career had exceeded his wildest dreams. He became president of the company and his income multiplied. They owned their own home instead of renting a two-bedroom apartment; they could afford to buy new furniture, new clothes, and even yearly vacations. But their tastes were still simple and Loretta still shopped with coupons. She saw no reason to spend frivolously just because they had more money. Their giving to the church had increased, and they now supported five missionaries instead of one.

There is no intrinsic virtue to being poor and struggling; on the other hand, neither is it a sure sign of God's blessing to being wealthy. God's concern is your heart; he is more interested in developing character in your life than in enlarging your bank account. The most important thing, now and always, is to love God with all your heart and to pass those values on to your children. Having money is not the issue. Loving God is.

Try this: *Tape a one-dollar bill to a piece of paper in the back of your Bible and write—on the bill or on the paper—"Money has its place, but God comes first." The visual reminder will help you to keep your prayers in proper perspective.*

GODLINESS WITH CONTENTMENT IS GREAT GAIN. FOR WE BROUGHT NOTHING INTO THE WORLD, AND WE CAN TAKE NOTHING OUT OF IT.

I TIMOTHY 6:6–7
NIV

COMMAND THOSE WHO ARE RICH TO PUT THEIR HOPE IN GOD. HE RICHLY PROVIDES US WITH EVERYTHING TO ENJOY.

I TIMOTHY 6:17
NIRV

Make all you can, save all you can, give all you can.

JOHN WESLEY

GOD IS ABLE

Hope deferred makes the heart sick, but a desire fulfilled is a tree of life.

~ Proverbs 13:12 NRSV

Roger and Melita's teenage daughter, Nicole, was part of the acting troupe in their church's youth group. She was excited when their church decided to send them to Europe during the summer holidays to perform skits and preach the gospel to local churches.

The church paid part of the troupe's expenses, but each teen still had to raise $2,500. Nicole found a job at a restaurant, but by June 1 she was still short. Roger and Melita contributed what they could, and wished they could help more, but couldn't."

Nicole sighed. "Maybe God doesn't want me to go."

"Don't give up hope," Roger said. "God will supply. Let's pray." A week later, a check arrived from Nicole's grandparents, and a friend from church donated some cash. By the time school was out, Nicole had enough money.

"We did it!" she laughed. "I wasn't sure that we could. Wow!"

"That's because we never stopped believing," Roger said. Thank you, God, he breathed.

Perseverance, hard work, self-sacrifice—these virtues are important, but all of them are built upon the foundation of hope. If you have hope and refuse to give up—whether you are struggling to send your kids to college or on a missions trip, trying to make a business succeed or praying for a child who isn't walking with God—hope is what will give you the strength to go the distance. The harder the struggle, the more enduring the hope you must have.

Try this: *Write your hopes for your children on a piece of card stock and attach it to the wall. If you want to send your kids on an outreach, add photos of the place. Post updates that show the progress you have made. Post obstacles such as "time" or "money" as prayer requests.*

May he give you the desire of your heart and make all your plans succeed.

Psalm 20:4 NIV

Give me strength, as you promised, and I shall live; don't let me be disappointed in my hope!

Psalm 119:116 GNT

Like one watching a glorious sunrise, so is a man who has waited long and prayed long, and finally sees his desire arrive.

Charles W. Foxe

Calm and Collected

Those who counsel peace have joy.

— *Proverbs 12:20* NRSV

Derek's son needed braces, but Derek's dental plan would only cover a small portion of the costs. His uncle Art counseled him to trust God, and Derek knew he was right. Then Art invited Derek and his two children to go sailing with him on his sailboat. "Get your mind off your problems," he said. Saturday morning came, and they set sail for the San Juan Islands.

They had nearly reached their destination when a freak squall broke, turning the sea dark and raising dangerous whitecaps. Art expertly trimmed the sails and turned on the engine, while Derek herded the kids to safety in the cabin. After half an hour of fighting wind and waves, they reached a small island where they waited out the storm.

That evening, Art told Derek, "For a landlubber, you sure were calm in that storm. You even helped me stay calm." He smiled.

Derek nodded. "God gave me peace because I placed my trust in him."

Having peace means having the ability to remain calm and peaceful in the midst of life's storms—no matter what they are or how uncertain the outcome. Being peaceful comes more naturally to some people, but for everyone it comes from a conscious decision to focus on God and trust him—even when you're battling worry, concern, or fear. When you go through a storm, commit your problems to God then allow him to fill your heart with peace.

Try this: *When you go through an unsettled or fearful time, pick a Scripture about God's peace that speaks clearly to you, type it on your computer, and print it out as a full-page poster. A good place to tape it would be the bathroom mirror or your refrigerator door.*

Those of steadfast mind you keep in peace—in peace because they trust in you.

Isaiah 26:3 NRSV

God's peace, which is far beyond human understanding, will keep your hearts and minds safe in union with Christ Jesus.

Philippians 4:7 GNT

Peace is the proper result of the Christian temper. It is the great kindness which our religion doth us, that it brings us to a settledness of mind.

Bishop Patrick

103

The Blessed Dad

Dad walked in the path of obedience
Though at first it was dusty and dry;
He rejoiced to obey for
he knew that one day
Blessings would rain from the sky.
He was merciful and
just and his God he loved,
He lacked nothing, and here is why:
The day came when blessings like soft,
gentle rain
Swept down on his
life from on high.

Ed Strauss

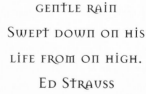

*Blessings are upon the
head of the just.*

~ *Proverbs* 10:6 KJV

*God said to Abraham,
"Through your
offspring all peoples on
earth will be blessed."*

~ *Acts* 3:25 NIV

Mountains
wrapped in
clouds do not
lack for rain;
nor do men who
love God lack
for blessings.

Arnold Chesterton

What's Enough?

Don't make me either poor or rich, but give me only the bread I need each day.

— *Proverbs 30:8 NIrV*

A CONTENTED MIND IS THE GREATEST BLESSING A MAN CAN ENJOY IN THIS LIFE.

JOSEPH ADDISON

Steve was thankful they had been able to afford this vacation—even if only barely. Their finances were very tight, but he and his wife, Karen, had planned and budgeted well. Steve, Karen, and their three children—Roy, Nancy, and Tim—had just spent a week tent-camping in Yellowstone National Park and were now driving through Montana to visit Karen's parents.

They stopped at a weather-beaten shop beside the road. A man showed them tables cluttered with dinosaur bones and fossil imprints in shale. When the man saw them excited about a trilobite fossil embedded in stone, he said, "It's yours for a hundred-fifty. That's the deal of a lifetime."

Steve and Karen stepped to the side and whispered animatedly. They decided Steve would try to bargain the price down. When that didn't work, they left the shop without it. "Sorry, kids. We just can't afford it."

"That's okay, dad," Roy replied. "I'm just happy we could come on this vacation."

"Me, too," Tim echoed.

It's difficult when you have to walk away from something you really want—whether it's a large-screen TV, a jacket, a car, a dream vacation, or some collector item. It's also difficult to tell your children they can't have what they want. Even if your finances were to increase dramatically, some things you desire will still be beyond your means. And just because you have the money doesn't mean you should buy something. This is why the Bible repeatedly says to be content with what you have.

TRY THIS: *Use a one-dollar Monopoly bill as a symbol of your trust in God. Put it in your billfold and pull it out to look at as needed. It may give your workmates a laugh, but it will also give you opportunity to show your faith.*

I HAVE LEARNED TO BE SATISFIED WITH WHAT I HAVE.

PHILIPPIANS 4:11 GNT

KEEP YOUR LIVES FREE FROM THE LOVE OF MONEY AND BE CONTENT WITH WHAT YOU HAVE.

HEBREWS 13:5 NIV

My God, give me neither poverty nor riches, but whatsoever it may be thy will to give, give me with it, a heart that knows humbly to acquiesce in what is thy will.

CHRISTIAN (GOTTHOLD) SCRIVER

Second Chances

The merciful man does himself good, but the cruel man does himself harm.

~ *Proverbs 11:17 NASB*

Carl had assured his boss he knew a particular CAD program, but when he failed to come through on a design for a complex machine part for a client, he found that there were huge gaps in his grasp of the software. He simply didn't know the program well enough, and the company lost the client as a result. Carl's boss came close to firing him, but decided at the last minute to give him another chance on the condition that Carl would learn the program thoroughly.

A month later, Carl's son Justin showed up at the house. Justin had played around in the eleventh grade and then dropped out of high school. Now he wanted to quit his job pumping gas, finish his studies, and move back home.

Their family's finances were tight, and Carl and his wife were unsure whether Justin had truly changed. But they decided it was important to make the sacrifice to give Justin another chance to finish his schooling.

᠅ Serious mistakes and failures to do things right stem from not being careful or concerned enough. Thank God that he doesn't throw the towel in on anyone. Thank God for mercy and for second chances! If you've ever failed at something important and have been given another opportunity to do things right, you probably learned to be thankful for mercy. Make a point to show that same mercy to others.

᠅ TRY THIS: *Zechariah 3:2 says the high priest is described as "a burning stick snatched from the fire." Take a partially burned stick from a fire, douse it in water, then nail that partially charred stick to your garage wall as a reminder that you yourself need mercy and should be merciful.*

THE LORD IS LONGSUFFERING, AND OF GREAT MERCY, FORGIVING INIQUITY AND TRANSGRESSION.

NUMBERS 14:18 KJV

BE MERCIFUL JUST AS YOUR FATHER IS MERCIFUL.

LUKE 6:36 GNT

He that has tasted the bitterness of sin fears to commit it; and he that hath felt the sweetness of mercy will fear to offend it.

WILLIAM COWPER

The Family Name

A good name is rather to be chosen than great riches.

~ *Proverbs 22:1* KJV

Allen Bjornsen's parents had owned a mom-and-pop grocery in a small Illinois farming town for decades, and the Bjornsens had established a great reputation in the community. Allen had spent years working in the store before moving to the city. Now he and his wife Linda had a young family and were ready for a change.

That's why, when his parents were ready to retire, Allen offered to take over the farm and store. It was a dream come true for both Allen and Linda. A month after moving to the old farmhouse, they were sitting leisurely around the breakfast table, nursing their second cup of coffee, when their daughter, Melody, exclaimed, "Every time I mention the name Bjornsen, people smile and then they ask me about Grandma and Grandpa!"

"My folks were extremely honest and fair," Allen said. "And generous. They knew everyone in the surrounding area, and everyone knew them. We're inheriting fifty years of good will."

110

The things you do, the things you say, how you say them, how you treat others, your attitude as you interact with people—these are vital building blocks in creating a good family name. As a father, strive to be kind, honest, and faithful each day of your life so that you will leave a good reputation for your children. Even if you have made mistakes in the past, you can start from where you are and make your name one they can be proud of.

TRY THIS: *Pencil the letters of your family name and then chisel them into a flat piece of wood. You may want to burn the letters or paint them with gold paint, or do both. Hang it in a prominent place in your house to remind you to do things that build up the worth of your name.*

I WILL MAKE YOUR NAME GREAT, AND YOU WILL BE A BLESSING.

GENESIS 12:2 NIV

A GOOD NAME IS BETTER THAN FINE PERFUME.

ECCLESIASTES 7:1 NIRV

A reputation for good judgment, fair dealing, truth, and rectitude, is itself a fortune.

HENRY W. BEECH

111

Fishing Buddies

Some friends play at friendship but a true friend sticks closer than one's nearest kin.

~ *Proverbs 18:24* NRSV

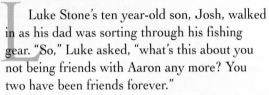

Life is to be fortified by many friendships. To love and be loved is the greatest happiness of existence.

Sydney Smith

Luke Stone's ten year-old son, Josh, walked in as his dad was sorting through his fishing gear. "So," Luke asked, "what's this about you not being friends with Aaron any more? You two have been friends forever."

Josh shrugged. "He's not cool any more. He wasn't good enough to make the baseball team. Plus he has a weird haircut this year."

"True friends don't dump friends," Luke said. "Friendship supercedes athletic ability or any hair style. Think about Sid Teleski and me. When we grew up we got different jobs and our interests changed, but we've stayed friends. When his truck rolled and he became paralyzed from the waist down, I was there for him. I stood by him and encouraged him because he's my friend."

"Yeah, but he can't do stuff with you anymore," Josh pointed out.

"Sure he can. We're going fishing together this afternoon. Do you want to come?"

Josh smiled. "Yeah."

You probably have many acquaintances and casual friends. The kind of friend you most likely desire, however, and the kind of friend you should be to others, is the friend who chooses your company and seeks you out to spend relaxing time. That ideal friend also sticks with you through hard times, when you're not so much fun to be with. If you have that kind of friend, value him. And be that kind of loyal friend to others.

Try this: If you've moved and had to leave good friends behind, find photographs of those friends and put them up. Your children will have left friends behind too. Ask them to do the same with their friends. Talk to them about your friends and listen to them talk about theirs.

A FRIEND LOVES AT ALL TIMES.

PROVERBS 17:17
NASB

DO NOT FORGET YOUR FRIENDS OR YOUR FATHER'S FRIENDS.

PROVERBS 27:10
GNT

The firmest friendships have been formed in mutual adversity; as iron is more strongly united by the fiercest flame.

CALEB C. COLTON

The Humble Dad

My dad was a quiet, humble man;

He never stood on a soapbox to boast—

Though he could've done that if he'd

wanted to

Since he'd managed to do more than most.

It wasn't his way to blow trumpets and say,

"Look at me, guys! Look what I've done!"

He just did what he did, and even as a kid

I was glad to be my father's son.

Ed Strauss

A humble spirit will obtain honor.

~ *Proverbs 29:23 NASB*

All of you, clothe yourselves with humility toward one another, for God is opposed to the proud, but gives grace to the humble.

~ *1 Peter 5:5 NASB*

Humility is the root, mother, nurse, foundation, and bond of all virtues.

John Chrysostom

Pleasing to God and Man

The upright enjoy God's favor.

~ Proverbs 14:9 NRSV

THE BEST
CHARACTERS ARE
MADE BY
VIGOROUS AND
PERSISTENT
RESISTANCE TO
EVIL TENDENCIES.

TIMOTHY DEXTER

Lorne Walters operated a welding shop. Lorne was a Christian and tried his best to operate his shop ethically. He had resolved years ago to treat his employees right and to serve his customers well. Lorne was also completely honest with his customers. It didn't take long before he had established a solid reputation.

Lorne often talked to his son, Chris, about the importance of godly character, but the lesson really came home one day when Chris was playing near the shop and a man and his son drove up. The boy walked over to watch Chris. "What are you doing?" he asked.

"Catching frogs," Chris answered. "Your dad need some welding done?"

The boy answered, "Yeah. We came here because everybody in town says to go to Walters Welding. They say he's the best welder in town and the most honest. Hey, why you grinning?

Chris grinned. "He's my dad."

Walking close to God, loving him, and obeying him pleases God and will, over time, transform your life. As your commitment to godly character grows, God's Spirit motivates you to deal honestly, considerately, and fairly with others. Jesus said that the first commandment was to love God wholeheartedly, and that the second was to love your neighbor as yourself. Make choices based upon sincere love for God and others, and consistently choose what is right.

Try this: *Pick an old wear-around-the-house T-shirt, grab a waterproof black marker, and write a slogan on it. Here are a couple suggestions: "Build Muscles, Build Character" "I'm a real character—and I want to develop more character!" Help your children come up with godly slogans for their T-shirts also.*

THE BOY SAMUEL CONTINUED TO GROW AND TO GAIN FAVOR BOTH WITH THE LORD AND WITH PEOPLE.

I SAMUEL 2:26 GNT

THE INTEGRITY OF THE UPRIGHT GUIDES THEM.

PROVERBS 11:3 NIV

To be worth anything, character must be capable of standing firm upon its feet in the world of daily work, temptation, and trial; and able to bear the wear and tear of actual life.

SAMUEL SMILES

117

A Small Gesture

What is desirable in a man is his kindness.

~ *Proverbs* 19:22 NASB

KIND LOOKS, KIND WORDS, KIND ACTS, AND WARM HANDSHAKES— THESE ARE SECONDARY MEANS OF GRACE WHEN MEN ARE IN TROUBLE.

JOHN HALL

As Nick and his daughter, Candace, arrived home from her dance practice, they saw a moving van in front the adjoining townhouse. The neighbors had told them that a family newly immigrated to the States was moving in. Nick saw that a man and a teenage boy were carrying a dresser down the ramp. The teen was having trouble carrying his end, so Nick immediately offered to help.

One night a week later, Nick was putting out garbage when he noticed the new neighbor's full barrels still under his carport. Nick knocked on the door and, when the man stuck his head out, asked, "Did you know tomorrow was garbage pickup day?" He hadn't known.

When Thanksgiving arrived Candace discovered that their new neighbors had never celebrated this holiday. After talking it over with her parents, she invited them over to share their feast.

"You are very kind," the neighbor's wife said. "I'm happy we moved to this neighborhood."

118

≈ Being considerate toward others and doing deeds of kindness usually only requires a small amount of time, and your actions show the motivation of your heart to do good. Thoughtful, meaningful deeds are often simply small, passing gestures throughout the day. It's important to teach your children to be kind to others, and it's even more important to show them by your own example. They're always watching you and, consciously or not, what you do every day teaches them how to be kind to others.

≈ TRY THIS: *When people need help, they often ask, "Can you spare a minute?" Set your wristwatch five minutes ahead of time so that when you're asked to lend a hand, you'll already have five minutes built into your schedule to help. Without boasting, be sure to tell your children stories of how you took a minute to help people.*

BE YE KIND ONE TO ANOTHER, TENDERHEARTED, FORGIVING ONE ANOTHER.

EPHESIANS 4:32 KJV

TO GODLINESS, ADD KINDNESS TO BELIEVERS. AND TO KINDNESS TO BELIEVERS, ADD LOVE.

2 PETER 1:7 NIRV

I expect to pass through life but once. If therefore, there be any kindness I can show . . . let me do it now, and not defer or neglect it, as I shall not pass this way again.

WILLIAM PENN

Clean Before God

Above all else, guard your heart, for it is the wellspring of life.

— *Proverbs 4:23* NIV

A CONSCIENCE
VOID OF
OFFENCE,
BEFORE GOD
AND MAN, IS AN
INHERITANCE
FOR ETERNITY.

DANIEL WEBSTER

Bill was on a business trip and was returning to his hotel room when he passed a magazine store. He stepped inside and was thumbing through an automotive magazine when the cover of an X-rated magazine caught his eye. The thought struck him: *No one in this city knows me.*

His heart began pounding. He was about to pick up the magazine when he stopped. *No, I can resist the temptation.* He bought a newspaper instead and left.

Seconds later his cell phone beeped. He flicked it on and his wife said, "Hi, hon. Tommy wants to talk to you." Seconds later Bill's son told his daddy that he had a fever and asked him to pray for him. Bill leaned against a streetlamp and prayed for his son's well being—and for his own, as well.

When he was finished, he talked with his wife briefly before signing off. He looked up at the sky and whispered, "Thanks, God."

It's important to have a clean conscience if you want to have the confidence that God will answer your prayers. Being right with God applies to your thoughts as well as to your acts. As a Christian, you have surrendered your life to God and allowed his Holy Spirit to transform your heart and mind. You will still be tempted, but when you make the right choices you remain in a right relationship with God. This gives you peace and opens your life to God's blessings.

Try this: If there's anything in your life that is not a good example to your children and doesn't honor God—whether it's an unpaid bill, unreturned tools, or unkept promises—deal with it right away, now if possible. If you have any unwholesome magazines, dump them in the trash. When you've finished, tell your kids that you've been "cleaning house."

THE PURPOSE OF THIS ORDER IS TO AROUSE THE LOVE THAT COMES FROM A PURE HEART, A CLEAR CONSCIENCE, AND A GENUINE FAITH.

1 TIMOTHY 1:5 GNT

BELOVED, IF OUR HEART CONDEMN US NOT, THEN HAVE WE CONFIDENCE TOWARD GOD.

1 JOHN 3:21 KJV

A good conscience is the palace of Christ; the temple of the Holy Ghost; the paradise of delight; the standing Sabbath of the saints.

SAINT AUGUSTINE

For Their Sakes

If you grow weak when trouble comes, your strength is very small.
— *Proverbs* 24:10 NIrV

Cecil was the owner of Thunder Hill Ranch. He had begun raising bison three years earlier when the price of beef couldn't keep the ranch financially afloat. It was either raise bison or move into town. But Cecil knew how much his two teenage daughters loved horseback riding and farm life, and so that pretty much made the decision for him.

Then the bison began getting sick. A week later the health inspector drove up and informed Cecil that he had to put the whole herd down. Cecil felt utterly defeated; it was just too much for him to handle. He wanted to give up, sell his acreage, and move into town.

Cecil walked to the top of Thunder Hill and prayed as he watched the sun set over the plains. An hour later he stepped into the house and told his daughters, "I've decided to hang on to the ranch. If we work very hard, we can build the herd back up."

Being a parent does a wonderful thing in your life—it means there are some things you can't do. This is a negative, yes, but it can also be a positive. For example, if you have children to consider, it isn't as easy to throw in the towel and admit defeat. Your responsibility toward your children puts extra muscle in your resolve to keep building the dream despite exhaustion and discouragement. After all, your children depend on you.

Try this: *If you have a picture of your wife and children in your wallet, attach a sticky note to it that reads, "You keep me going. I'll be strong for your sakes." When you're discouraged, take it out, look at their faces, and pray for God's strength.*

I WILL GO IN THE STRENGTH OF THE LORD GOD.

Psalm 71:16 KJV

THOSE WHO TRUST IN THE LORD FOR HELP WILL FIND THEIR STRENGTH RENEWED.

Isaiah 40:31 GNT

We have but to toil awhile, endure awhile, believe always, and never turn back.

William G. Simms

The Diligent Dad

A customer raced through
my dad's garage door.
"I need my engine tuned
and I need it by four."
At four the man jumped up
and said with a wheeze,
"Did you finish?" Dad nodded
and gave him his keys. . . .
Did dad leave any deeds undone?
Not a chance!
Ed Strauss

The desires of the diligent are fully satisfied.

~ *Proverbs* 13:4 *NIV*

The plans of the diligent lead surely to abundance.

~ *Proverbs* 21:5 *NRSV*

DILIGENCE IS THE MOTHER OF GOOD FORTUNE, AND IDLENESS, ITS OPPOSITE, NEVER LED TO GOOD INTENTION'S GOAL.

MIGUEL DE CERVANTES

At Inspirio we love to hear from you—your
stories, your feedback,
and your product ideas.
Please send your comments to us
by way of e-mail at
icares@zondervan.com
or to the address below:

inspirio

Attn: Inspirio Cares
5300 Patterson Avenue SE
Grand Rapids, MI 49530

If you would like further information
about Inspirio and the products we
create please visit us at:
www.inspiriogifts.com

Thank you and God Bless!